10 EPIC WAYS TO BE A

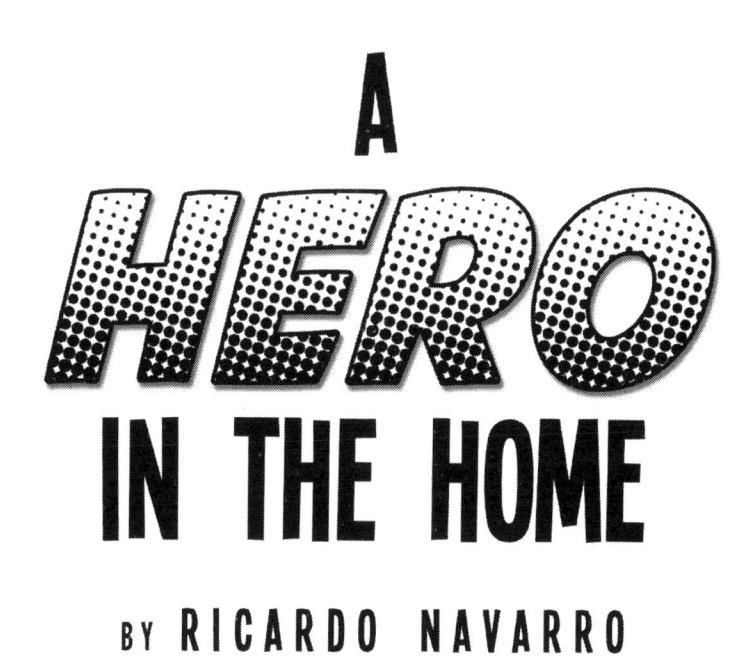

A HERO IN THE HOME

BY RICARDO NAVARRO

www.THECRAZYCHRISTIANBLOG.com

A Hero in the Home: 10 Epic Ways to be a Better Dad
Published by Navarro Family Publishing and The Crazy Christian Blog
TheCrazyChristianBlog@gmail.com
ISBN-13: 978-1514249000
ISBN-10: 1514249006

Scripture quotations are from the ESV® Bible (The Holy Bible, English Standard Version®), copyright © 2001 by Crossway, a publishing ministry of Good News Publishers. Used by permission. All rights reserved.

All other written material Copyright © 2015 Ricardo Navarro for Navarro Family Publishing. All rights reserved. No part of this publication may be reproduced, distributed, or transmitted in any form or by any means, including photocopying, recording, or other electronic or mechanical methods, without the prior written permission of the publisher, except in the case of brief quotations embodied in critical reviews and certain other noncommercial uses permitted by copyright law. All other rights reserved.

TABLE OF CONTENTS

Biblical Fatherhood, How the Heroes of the past did it.	13
Luke Skywalk had Daddy issues and so did I.	27
Time to man up, Turn your G.I. JANE into G.I. Joe.	37
Save YOUR heroine in distress, Prioritizing your leading lady.	47
Keep your legacy intact, Let the Force be strong in you.	57
Reach Back and pass Forward, You have much to learn Grasshopper you also have much to give.	67
Initiate, Instigate and Agitate, Time to Smash!	77
Show up and Show out, Heroes Save the day.	93
Make the Tough Calls, With Great Power comes Great Responsibility.	101
Don,t Take Time, Create time, Being RIGHT on time.	113
Be the Dad You Didn,t Have Don't Be the Villain.	123
Be A Gentleness Giant, Less is truly more.	133
What NOT to do, Kryptonite Alert	145
A League of Extraordinary Gentlemen Surrender it all at the cross.	159

DEDICATIONS

This book is dedicated to Milly Himmelright and Elba Cherry. You guys planted a seed a long time ago and it never died. Thank you for your faithfulness and ability to see past the foolishness of youth into the greatness of God's potential in a young person's life.

This book is also dedicated to my mother Silvia Navarro. If there is legacy in my children, it is because of you. Because of a woman, I know what it is to be a man and for that irony I am grateful. In you I found the perfect example of a life submitted to Christ being able to do great things in spite of the circumstances that surround them. You were the hero in my home and I am eternally indebted to you. Your happiness brings me great joy and you deserve to be called "Nona".

This book is also dedicated to my father Felix Navarro. He passed away one month before this book was finished and he never got to read it. That part makes me sad. However, the part that makes me happy is that he saw this book lived out in my life and it changed his for the better. I will always love you Papi.

This book is dedicated to the many warriors I have had the pleasure of doing life with. These are the men whose awesome example and dedication to living out God's call on their lives, has left an everlasting impression on mine. From pastors to roommates and sometimes pastors who were roommates, you guys are the ones that remind me that "the good ones" are still out there. You guys were the inspiration I needed to get through the constant voices of discouragement I heard while writing this book. It is not your perfection that shines, but your dedication to being the best men you can be in spite of your flaws that I will always be driven by. I am grateful to call you friend and honored to be your brother.

Finally, this book is dedicated to my children. The Lord spoke to me when I was 21 years old and told me that I would have each of you specifically. He told me I would father a few boys, a girl that was only partially my own and here you all are. It is amazing to see God's faithfulness in fruition. Because of you guys, this book exists and for you, this book was created because I want each of you to know the God who created you and how to lead in your own home one day. I love each of you deeply.

UP, UP, AND AWAY!
INTRODUCTION

Dads are like built-in superheroes in a person's life. In addition to being impervious to harm, faster than a train and able to dodge bullets, there are no broken machines that cannot be fixed, no refrigerators too heavy to lift and no jar lid too tight that has a chance of not being decimated by the sheer strength of a dad's iron hands. This guy is amazing. Growing up you may have wanted to be just like him. I mean this guy has more swag than Pepé Le Pew and the romantic chops to back it up. He loves his wife and she loves him with an adoring respect and great admiration. He spends all his free time with his kids, building tree houses with the boys and sipping tea with his little girls. He makes stacks of cash, is handsome and is fashionably sensible, at least most of the time, and he has an impeccable sense of direction. He is downright just amazing. Everyones dad is like this right? No? Maybe he wasn't all of these things but surely some parts.

I know I am painting an exaggerated picture but isn't it the picture of what a perfect dad is supposed to look like? In fact, this masterpiece of a man is the guy we as men hope to be one day. If you had a dad that you considered a good one, then you have a head start. However, if you had a dad who wasn't even close to this description, and I think most would fall into the latter category, then what are you supposed to do? What if you had a dad and he was just "OK"? These types of dads come with varying amounts of good and bad and are what probably most of us grew up with. This is the type of dad who was there in the flesh but was not there in the mind or spirit. Sure, he was generally a good man. He paid his bills on time and made an effort to love his family but there was something missing. Something was not right and it was just below the surface. This type of father had his intentions in the right place but found it easier to avoid responsibility than to own it. Maybe he drank too much. Maybe he had a secret stash of porn that he would escape to, maybe his escape was smoking a little weed or a cigarette when no one was around. Maybe he would escape the realities of his wife and children by diving into work a little more than he needed to, sound familiar? He worked hard and deserved a little fun every now and again but when it came down to needing a solid back bone this was not your guy. Sure you had 185 plus pounds of man meat in front of you but when it came time to engage, time to love and discipline, this guy might as well have been an oasis in the desert. He was visibly present, but emotionally an illusion.

What then? What are you supposed to do with this guy? How did that shape you and what you want to be? This is the weak and unintelligent father played on so many TV shows. I think it's the prevailing image that most of society has about the role of fatherhood and the men who play in that role. However, who is really to blame for that notion when most men, are in fact, disengaging from their God given responsibilities? Maybe all the jars in your house could be easily opened but when you needed him to open the containers of your heart, the places that only a dad could open, those strong arms and hands were diminished to noodle-like strength. Moreover when it came to manning up and making the tough calls, this dad was nowhere to be found. You would not call this dad a bad dad, but you wouldn't call him a good one either. What do you do with that? How do you build the house of fatherhood and live out manhood in your own life when this guy was the foundation that you started with?

I mean maybe dad wasn't a deadbeat but he wasn't a pillar of strength either. Maybe he was just "all right" or not around at all and your view of manhood is non-existent because of it and right now you are trying to figure what "being a man" is all about. This may have been for any number of reasons but, based on stats at the time of this writing, I am willing to say that the majority of fatherless homes are a result of choice, choices made by him or her, circumstances and or divorces that made having a family seem impossible. All that being said you lie somewhere in the middle, the product of a broken home. Manly strength and guidance was missing from your upbringing leaving you to figure out what male strength exactly is and how it should be played out in life. This left you in one of two ways; either with an emptiness inside which has sent you on a lifelong quest to try to fill that void with an innumerable amount of other things, or indifferent, which, in all reality, is probably just like having a void only this time with an added side of anger to mask that fact that you care. Inevitably, many jars in your homes were reduced to being pried open with a butter knife in Dad's absence. Don't get me wrong, so many mothers, my own included, are superwomen in their own right, but there is no denying that dads have a special place in life and the absence of their role is supremely missed and needed. In fact, a father's impact in life is so instrumental and so desperately needed that many of us, for the durations of our lives, carry a place in our heart for our fathers even if they weren't around and even if they didn't come close to resembling any kind of hero.

Since the introduction of sin into the world, men, in particular, have been trying to figure out their role on the earth. What was immediately obvious is that out of the two sexes, we tend to be bigger, faster, and stronger and we have been using these traits to our advantage ever since. Men have abused power and position since the beginning. We have abused it in our roles as providers, leaders and protectors. We have used it for selfish gain, political dominance, and deadly force both physically and emotionally.

Throughout the course of history we have seen this story play out in many ways. At the center of every man-made, globally catastrophic event that affects all of humanity, there usually lies a man. From the Caesars to Hitler to Bin Laden, there has always been, at the forefront, a man whose role and influence is affecting millions of people. I can't even think of one woman who has had a similar catastrophic influence to these men. That's not to say that there aren't women who have had a crucial role to play in human history, but what I am saying is that, in my opinion, there has not been one woman who has, on a global scale, had the same direct and negative influence on the history of humanity. It is always, for some reason, a man. Though the destruction caused by these men is a horrific stain on the history of humanity there are similar atrocities being committed every day albeit on a much smaller scale. In homes across the globe, the next generation of children are being raised under similar travesties where the man of the house is living out his rule as a tyrant. Some could even argue that the effects of this type of upbringing are just as devastating over time as any of the world's greatest man-made catastrophes. I believe there is a gross misunderstanding of the position and authority of manhood. This has led many men to take advantage of their God-given asset of strength in a way that does not build up but tears down.

Though in the modern era we are not predominantly ruled by kings or dictators, you could say that they still exist. Today's kings are those who are celebrated in the public eye and whose influence is over culture as a whole. People in this category range from movie stars, musicians, and professional athletes to politicians and media-moguls. However, thinking that this exertion of power is only seen at a macro level is also misguided. The same power that brings each of these men into these positions lies in the heart of every man who walks the earth. The manifestation of this power varies, but the potential exists.

The anointing of manhood is a powerful force that is duplicitous in nature. It comes with many responsibilities and has power to affect lives in both positive and negative ways. Any powerful force out of control can destroy life. A fire, for example, in the wrong place can destroy, but in a good place can provide warmth and nourishment. Similarly, having children puts you in a place of great influence over the lives of your kids. It also stands to shape the lives that they will touch as a result of the influence that you have had in their life. So what you do with that influence matters.

There are few things more sobering than looking into the eyes of your child and recognizing your own mortality. By the grace of God, this child will outlive you so if you are paying attention, you realize that the birth of a child marks the countdown to your own life's end. This makes what you instill in this child all the more important if you desire your legacy to live on in a positive light. For some, the idea of legacy has no bearing on how they decide to live life, this is especially noticeable in the generations of young people who no longer desire to have children. Yet for others who find significance in leaving a heritage, the values they leave behind in the lives of their children give them a great sense of purpose.

So what will you do with all that you know about being a man? Will you rise up and be the hero in your home that God has called you to be? Will you destroy any jammed jar lid be it in the physical world or be it in the heart? Or will you cower in defeat, like so many before you, only to use your strength to destroy instead of building up? I hope it's not the latter.

I don't know many good men who aren't at the very least intrigued by a challenge to their manhood. That being the case, I am glad you are here. You see, there is nothing wrong with not being equipped to do the job of being a dad. As I have already mentioned, your example may have left you with a lack-luster start. But there is everything wrong with staying unequipped in fatherhood and that's what I want to try to help you with.

In the following pages I want to outline a few things that will help guide you on your journey to not only "becoming a man" but to becoming the "father" that God wants you to be. These are some of the things that I have learned along this journey that I am still on. They are simple truths that have helped me tremendously and I believe they will help you become the hero in your home that you are supposed to be.

> *"Hear, O sons, a father's instruction, and be attentive, that you may gain insight...Hear, my son, and accept my words, that the years of your life may be many."*
> *Proverbs 4:1,10*

CHAPTER ONE
BIBLICAL FATHERHOOD
HOW THE HEROES OF THE PAST DID IT.

There are a few different definitions of fatherhood depending on where you are in the world as well as many different circumstances that can lead a man to claiming this title. There is the traditional understanding, that is by way of impregnating a female counterpart, also known as "biological fatherhood". This is the one that comes to mind almost immediately when I think of the term, as I am sure it does for you as well. However, the topic of fatherhood is much broader than mere biological donations will allow for. Much like the difference of having a wedding versus having a marriage; being a dad, or at least a good one, is much more than a one-time event that leads to the commencement of a human life. The truth is that any physically mature man, biologically at least, can become a dad but only an elite few succeed at being fathers.

The word "father" almost always refers to a man but doesn't only mean a man who has created a child. Some of the other definitions of the word "father" state the following:

- One who originates or institutes
- One who protects and gives protection

- Spiritual leadership or mentorship

As we can see here, it's not limited to creating a life. It actually has more to do with the on-going role that a man can play in a person's or an organization's life.

There are several great examples of both good and bad fathering found in the Bible. I want to look at a handful of these men and the lives they lead as fathers and see if we can't learn a thing or two from their successes and their failures as men and as fathers. Let's see if we can't take away some nuggets of truth that will help to strengthen our desire to be better fathers.

THE FIRST DAD

First up, God. The one with a capital "G". A.KA. "The author and the finisher", "the beginning and the end", "the King of Kings and Lord of Lords". The "great I AM". I love this last description, though for many years the definition eluded me. It means that He is constant. He always was and always will be. When I think of the ultimate father and father of fathers, I can't help but think about God. He is the originator and father of all things and He exemplifies every definition through and through. The whole concept of fatherhood begins and ends with Him.

In the Bible there are over 1600 mentions of the word "father" in all sorts of contexts. I would say that this is an indication of how important the role of fatherhood is to God. From cover to cover, there are stories about God's love, discipline, and redemption shown towards His children. Also we get to see the ultimate parent-child relationship demonstrated in the life of Christ. This illustration gives us an up close and personal view on how God loves those who claim Him to be their father and even those who don't. God's possessive and parenting natures are evident right from the beginning of the book.

In the first three chapters of the first book of the Bible, God is establishing the institution of fatherhood right out of the gate. It is literally the first thing He does in biblical recorded history. He becomes, for all intents and purposes, a father. In Genesis, God creates the environment (authorship, founder, originator), provides food and shelter (provision), gives life to Adam and Eve and sets forth the rules and regulations of a perfect life on the earth (protection), thus beginning His relationship with all of His creation. It was perfect. It's probably safe to assume that if Adam and Eve had not fallen, the role of fatherhood and manhood would to this day remain unmarred.

As men, if we can learn to see God as our heavenly Father who gives us strength, provides for and protects us, especially if we did not have an earthly father, it can give our lives a whole new set of purposes and direction. As human men, who inherently bear the weight of their circumstances on their shoulders, we can easily become bogged down with the cares of family and finances. However, if we can learn to stay plugged into the constant source of strength, wisdom, and hope that comes from our heavenly father, then our lack of resources on this earth will not matter as much, the strength of our shoulders will be irrelevant and our future will be firmly assured in the promises that He gives us. If you want to learn how to be a superhero in your home, you must learn the lessons that are given out by the hero of heroes. Many of them are difficult to digest and you may want to bow out of the race, but when your teacher is omnipotent (all-powerful), omniscient (all-knowing), and omnipresent (everywhere), where can you go that He will not see you? Where can you run to that will allow you to hide? What duty can you abandon that He is not aware of? While these attributes are true of His nature He is also your advocate who desires nothing more than for you to succeed in the time and the endeavors He has given you. This includes being a dad. You may have thought it was an accident that you are now in the role of being a father but in God's eyes, there was no accident. You may be trying to become a biological father without success and are wondering if being a dad is even in God's plan for you but I assure you already have been given the title! So you should take great pride in knowing that the one who has assigned you the role of father greatly believes in you and in the strength that He provides for you to succeed in your position.

God the father is the greatest example of fatherhood and when there is any question of what to do or who to look at for an example of fathering, His demonstration is more than sufficient, especially if you didn't have an example to look to. He actually specialized in being "a father to the fatherless." Psalms 68:5. There is so much to say about that alone that a human lifetime is not a sufficient amount of time to learn all there is about His incredible character, but the Bible is a great place to start. There have also been many other books throughout the ages written about the character of God. There are still many to be written as He is constantly revealing Himself anew to every generation. This is probably one of my favorite characteristics of God the father. Though in Him is great holiness, He is incredibly merciful and patient with how feeble every generation of humanity is. He shows this mercy by revealing Himself to each of these generations in a unique and special way. We are finite men, often without a clear view on who this God is and yet He desires for us to know Him. In spite of our open and vehement rejection of His decrees for humanity, He lets us breathe, He lets us create and prosper. He pursues us as a gentleman would, not forcing Himself on us, even though, as a father, He has every right to impose His will. He is the ultimate dad.

THE FIRST DAD TO MESS UP

The next major father figure we can look at is also the next major father in chronological time. Adam is an incredible person to study. He was the first zoologist, the first horticulturist and the first human man. He was also the only man without a mother and a father. Being the only man on the planet must have come with its pros and cons. Being close to the Creator would have definitely been the biggest pro but being the only human could easily be seen as being a bit of a drag, hence a tick in the con category.

Adam's only role model in being a father was God and yet he still had many failures as a man. I think sometimes we can look at God and know that He is our ultimate example of fatherhood but feel overwhelmed by aspiring to His greatness. We can sometimes think, "Trying to be like God is impossible, so why even try?" However it is interesting to see the line of misfits in the Bible, one right after the other, that God chooses to tell His story and they all begin with Adam. He was the first one to get it wrong right out of the gate, even with God walking with him, literally side by side.

From Adam's example we can learn a few things. First, we must learn that we are weak and that relying on our own strength, even when we are capable, will sometimes yield a negative result. However, when we do mess up we must own our responsibility head on. Adam's first sin was to neglect his responsibility as a leader and a father of the Garden of Eden, however the very next sin was the sin that I think is a deathblow to all humankind even to this day. That was that he made an excuse. Adam's attempt to make an excuse for his sin was his effort to convince God that he had done nothing wrong but the blame was actually God's to claim. Imagine trying to convince the all-knowing creator of all things that He is wrong. Remember He knows everything, even before it happens; He is all-powerful and everywhere at once. Nice try, Adam, but not a chance. Adam was mistaken in many ways but you could say that this was his greatest error and I would say it is our error as well.

Since then, many men have been neglecting their responsibilities and making excuses for the results. As a consequence, we have all been greatly impacted. This is seen clearly in fathers who are neglectful of their wives and children or in young men who father children but do not take care of the responsibility of raising them well, if at all. The order of life was disrupted when Adam allowed Eve to be deceived. It was a major failure in his strength as a leader. When Adam decided to make excuses for the failure he had committed, he set a certain chain of reactions in motion that would affect every living organism and every relationship from then on throughout the rest of history. It is pretty profound to think of it in that light. Our role as fathers affect absolutely everything in our sphere of influence and continue to do so for generations after the decisions have been made.

THE CRAZY DAD

Noah is another amazing father. The "Noah" movie that came out in 2014 portrays the character Noah as a man on a mission who has gone mad in his effort to complete his task. Though much of the story was recreated for entertainment purposes, I found parts of the depiction quite plausible. Love or hate the movie, it will definitely force you to imagine yourself in the sandals of Noah and the job that he was given to accomplish.

SPOILER ALERT! In the movie, the picture that is painted is of a man gone mad by God-given visions of the earth's destruction. His task is to build an ark to save the animals. This also coincides with the only reason his family is being spared. They would be charged with the task of saving the animals but then, once that was done, they too would die off leaving creation alone to fix itself without the interference of humanity's evil. Noah's task would be to see that through no matter what the cost. (On a side note, notice the subtle but present underlying message from Hollywood, that people who believe in this God, do crazy and illogical things and should not be trusted.) In the movie, Noah had to be willing to kill his own family if they stood in the way of God's plan and, though I don't think that was the most biblically accurate portion of the Noah movie, the determination of a man to be obedient to God is the real story that we can learn from.

Noah could be considered the second father of mankind, responsible for the second beginning of the population after the flood. Noah was also an architectural engineer and ship maker who was given the task to build a structure that had never been built before in the history of mankind. These would have been marvels even in our day and age. However, more than these things, Noah was also the last man of a generation to still have faith in God. We can't forget this because it was this fact that triggered the flood in the first place. The world that Noah lived in was said to be completely and utterly wicked but Noah was found to be "righteous" and "blameless". What is interesting is that the text does not say that he was sinless or perfect, but that he loved God and was committed to obedience. In an environment that was anti-God and against all that Noah stood for, Noah found the strength to stand on his own in the midst of a wicked generation and be the man that God called him to be. This allowed him to lead his family to safety and kept his legacy intact. Whether this story actually occurred in human history is not as important as the lessons that we can learn from it. As men and as fathers we must be incredibly committed to obedience to God against all odds in order for our families to thrive and flourish in the plans that He has uniquely created for each and every one of us.

THE REST OF THE GANG

I have given you three examples of fatherhood so far. Let me briefly summarize some of the other lessons we can learn from key figures in the Bible. How many children do you have? One? Two? Ten? What if you were responsible for fathering a whole nation? Abraham is known as the father of the Jewish nation and, like the others, God found him to be qualified for the task in spite of his own shortcomings. Abraham relied on his own strength and understanding, he faltered and the repercussions were severe. After God promised Abraham a son in his old age, his wife, Sarah, did not see it possible. So at her suggestion, Abraham impregnated one of his servant girls. Some believe that the result of that union, a son name Ishmael, is the cause of the religion of Islam today. Sweet! Thanks for that gem of a contribution, Abraham. Not that I have anything against Islam, aside from the terrorism or the fact that I don't believe it to be true. What I am more specifically referring to, are the thousands of years of conflict in the region as a result. According to the Bible, the son that Abraham was supposed to have with Sarah was Isaac not Ishmael, but because Ishmael was born first, which was a highly coveted position in eastern culture, problems have been ensuing ever since. Whether or not this particular part of the story is true or not, we don't know. What we DO know is that there are great repercussions for not being obedient to the instructions God has given.

Isaac was another interesting father to look at. He could have been a son living in the shadow of a great father. Some men feel like they have to live up to the example that was set by the men in their lives who they respect. Though this may ring true in some ways, we, like Isaac, must learn to be the unique and individual men that God has called us to be. Another one of Isaac's outstanding qualities would be that he never grew resentful of the fact that his father Abraham almost killed him. He never blamed God but continued to serve Him faithfully and would be known as a faithful follower of God. Isaac was also known for being faithful to only one wife, which, in an age of polygamy, would have been a rare quality. Isaac was not perfect though. He favored his son Esau, which would later cause division in his home. You could say the trait was passed on when Jacob, Isaac's other son, would do the same thing with his son Joseph. By favoring Joseph, Jacob would stir up jealousy in his ten other sons who would then plot against Joseph to get rid of him by faking his death. The falling dominoes can potentially never end if fathers do not remain tapped into obedience.

Moses would bear the weight of delivering a whole race of people out of oppressive rule. He would also have to be strong enough to deliver and carry out Jewish Law—something that had also never been done before. His faults? He stuttered and had issues trusting God when it counted. The result was his admission to the Promised Land would be revoked. King David, though loved and favored by God, would struggle greatly with lust that eventually would lead to murder. He was strong in battle but sometimes absent as a father. Through all of this God calls him a man after his own heart. He is a perfect example of a man whose heart belongs to God but his actions did not necessarily always line up with his heart. Did I mention that David's sons were a hot mess too? He passed all of his traits, both positive and negative and then some, on to his boys, all of which affected the whole kingdom of Israel. Joseph, Jesus' earthly father, is probably one of the most underrated fathers in the Bible. How would you like the responsibility of raising and taking care of the physical manifestation of God, never mind trying to teach him stuff he probably already knew? I am sure that it was not an easy job to "correct" the Creator of all things who was asleep in the other room. His title of father was handed to him outside of his own doing, which, in his day would have had its own implications. So in one sense he was forced to deal with owning a child who was physically not his own. He would have faced ridicule for staying with Mary and had not an angel spoken to him about his duty, he more than likely would have quit the position to avoid the shame, but, like a boss, he stuck it out. He owned it and trusted that God's plan was in play. The Bible doesn't say much about the weaknesses of Joseph but I am sure it is pretty safe to say he had them and fear was probably right up there. What we can learn from him is that trusting in God's plan in spite of how dire a situation may look is always a great plan of action.

I think it is safe to look at these examples and see that these men were indeed just men, champions in one moment and losers the next. However, the common thread that runs through them all is a deep and profound trust in the God that they all served. Their examples stand to teach us all what we need as fathers and, though I only scraped the surface of each of their lives, we can learn to be better fathers as a result of both their successes and failures. Other fathers in the Bible worth checking out would be guys like Jonadab and Job. See 2 Kings 10:15-16, Jer. 35:1-1, Jer. 35:12-14, Jer. 35:18-19, also the book of Job.

THE ABSENT DADS

There are also some examples of fatherhood in the Bible that stand as a warning to us. These men were so incredibly wicked that most of us would look at their example and say, "There's no way I would ever do that," or "I'm nowhere near that bad." And though we must be careful to avoid being like these examples on the outside, we must also be sure our hearts are not disengaged on the inside. The Bible actually tells a lot about the failures of fathers, which within itself is worth noticing, but let's look at the lives of fathers that the Bible deems as wicked.

Eli and Samuel come to mind when thinking about the repercussions of poor fathering. Eli's sons were supposed to be priests endowed with all the priestly rights and prestige of that position in that day. It was a sacred position that should have been held with honor and a deep respect for being entrusted with it. However, they took advantage of God's people by extortion and were also known to be having sexual relations with women who worked at the temple. Pastors sleeping with their secretaries. Sound familiar? Not so very different from the stories we hear in our day and age. Now here is where Eli's poor fathering comes into play. The Bible tells of a simple rebuke that Eli gives to his sons but by then it was too late. Good job, Eli! That slap on the hand for bedding the temple girls will really show them who's boss! Way to hold it down like a "G"! The problem was that it didn't. Eli's sons' actions actually beg the question of where Eli was during the upbringing of these boys.

The Bible says that Eli was a high priest so it's safe to assume that he was caught up in priestly duties. He was too busy with work (church work at that, pay attention full-time ministers) to realize that his own home was in disarray. Sound familiar? It ties back to Adam's story—neglect then excuse. It is easy for the man to shove off the duty of fatherhood in the name of providing and making money, but the job of provision is not only limited to the financial realm; it is all-inclusive, meaning that a father's position includes financial provision but is not limited to it. A father's provision comes in the form of emotional and spiritual provision as well. Eli was not around to be the fatherly influence that he should have been to his sons and, as a result, these boys brought great shame and ultimately death to themselves and their father. Eli's rebuke fell on deaf ears because it was too late to become the father he should have already been.

The Bible says that Eli's rebuke was not heard because God had already decided that He was going to kill them. Bet that temple tail didn't look so good then. This would eventually fall back on Eli himself when later the enemies of Israel would slaughter thousands. Eli's sons were a part of the many who were killed. This news, along with the Ark of the Covenant, a sacred altar, being stolen, would send Eli over the edge of a chair where he broke his neck.

The irony of this story lies not in the fate of the sons of Eli and Eli himself, however; it lies in Samuel. Samuel was a young boy who was entrusted to Eli's care at a young age to be a servant in the temple. Samuel would grow up to be a prophet over the people of Israel for many years and was, in fact, the same prophet who prophesied to Eli exactly what would happen to him and his sons. Yet Samuel's own sons would also be seen as inadequate to serve in the House of the Lord. The Bible says that they did not "walk in the same ways" as Samuel and that "they perverted justice". So if Samuel was the prophet who gave Eli the verdict on his life as a result of his poor fathering, why didn't Samuel himself get the message that being a present father was important? As a result, his own sons fell away from the Lord.

Eli and Samuel were good men, God-fearing men who had issues with their children. On one hand it is easy to look at their lives and condemn them for being poor fathers, but then, on the other hand, it just goes to show you that even men with a heart after God can fail in the area of fathering. It is not an easy task and it is something that we need to be seeking God's wisdom for on a daily basis. Job would actually get up early and send for his children to pray over them and to make sacrifices on their behalf. He did this just in case there was any sin or wickedness in their heart against God. "Perhaps my sons have sinned and cursed God in their hearts." "This Job did continually." (Job 1:4–5) How much more should we be doing for our children in this day and age where their access to anything and everything is only a few clicks away?

Manassah was only twelve years old when he came into rule, which would present its own set of problems, I am sure. However, he was known for rejecting God in openly defiant ways. He rebuilt torn down temples that were dedicated to other gods and worshiped them there. The stones on this guy! The Bible also says he had the gall to build these same altars in the temple. It was almost like a slap in the face to the God of Israel. He also made his sons "pass through the fire", practiced witchcraft, used divination and dealt with mediums and spiritists. The Bible says that he did "much evil in the sight of the Lord provoking him to anger." I don't know about you but I do not want to provoke the God of Creation to any kind of anger! That's just not the God you mess with. The God of Israel had a long track record of dealing with His people in a very public and over-the-top fashion, so you would think that openly defying Him was probably not a good idea, but it goes to show you that when you think you have it under control and you are trusting in your own ability to see things clearly, you could be treading on dangerous waters. Again, you might not be trying to sacrifice your kids to demon gods (2 Kings 21:1-9) but your lack of presence in their lives may be allowing them to be exposed to demons that would love nothing more than to take them from you.

Be on the lookout! These stories of biblical men and how they handled fatherhood are just as relevant today as they were when the stories were written down. The attack on family is real and you are at the helm. If you are not, then who is steering the ship? The tides of culture? Cultural currents are always deliberately pushing in a direction that is opposite to the direction of God's will for your life, so if you are withdrawn from your position of fatherhood, thinking that it doesn't matter, you should know that your family is on a crash course with the rocks that life will surely bring. The enemy would love nothing more than to undermine your God-given authority. Do not make it easy for him to do it by not even being present.

This chapter begins with God being the ultimate example of fatherhood and I will end it on that same thought. While there is no father like Him, there are many who are trying to be. I consider you to be one of them. If we want to be great dads, we have to learn how to be obedient children who spend time with their father learning about how He wants us to be so we can eventually pass the lessons on. Psalm 103 is an incredible reminder of God's fatherly love toward His children and it also stands as an example that we can look to when we are looking for biblical example of how to love our children.

Psalm 103:1-18 says:

> *Bless the Lord, O my soul,*
>   *and all that is within me,*
>   *bless his holy name!*
> 2
> *Bless the Lord, O my soul,*
>   *and forget not all his benefits,*
> 3
> *who forgives all your iniquity,*
>   *who heals all your diseases,*
> 4
> *who redeems your life from the pit,*
>   *who crowns you with steadfast love and mercy,*
> 5
> *who satisfies you with good*
>   *so that your youth is renewed like the eagle's.*
> 6
> *The Lord works righteousness*
>   *and justice for all who are oppressed.*
> 7
> *He made known his ways to Moses,*
>   *his acts to the people of Israel.*
> 8
> *The Lord is merciful and gracious,*
>   *slow to anger and abounding in steadfast love.*
> 9
> *He will not always chide,*

> *nor will he keep his anger forever.*
>
> 10
> *He does not deal with us according to our sins,*
>   *nor repay us according to our iniquities.*
>
> 11
> *For as high as the heavens are above the earth,*
>   *so great is his steadfast love toward those who fear him;*
>
> 12
> *as far as the east is from the west,*
>   *so far does he remove our transgressions from us.*
>
> 13
> *As a father shows compassion to his children,*
>   *so the Lord shows compassion to those who fear him.*
>
> 14
> *For he knows our frame;*
>   *he remembers that we are dust.*
>
> 15
> *As for man, his days are like grass;*
>   *he flourishes like a flower of the field;*
>
> 16
> *for the wind passes over it, and it is gone,*
>   *and its place knows it no more.*
>
> 17
> *But the steadfast love of the Lord is from everlasting to everlasting on those who fear him,*
>   *and his righteousness to children's children,*
>
> 18
> *to those who keep his covenant*
>   *and remember to do his commandments.*

CHAPTER TWO
LUKE SKYWALKER HAD DADDY ISSUES
AND SO DID I.

    I am not sure when I realized that perfection wasn't my dad's middle name. I think it was a gradual eroding that began to happen somewhere in my teens. When I got tired of looking into the stands at some sporting event and not seeing him there, the lights came on. In reality to this day I can't remember him at many athletic events even though I played sports throughout my entire childhood. I also can't remember him at many other important events in my life like birthdays, my wedding or the births of my children, though by then I had gotten so used to it that it wasn't even an afterthought. My dad did come to a few things that were so few and far apart that he might as well have not been there at all.

    Even still I wouldn't consider my dad a "bad" dad. I would consider him an "in-between dad," not great but not bad either. A good man who was well intended but lacked execution when it counted. My earliest recollections of my father were of him leaving and coming home from work tired, eating, and going to sleep. I recall the sleep part in particular because first, I don't remember him and my mom sleeping in the same room and second, the sleeping part was mind blowingly loud. Like ear-shattering loud; like the sound of gravel being tossed in a dryer that was attached to a PA system cranked all the way up. His snoring was unforgettable. I also remember Saturdays being very special because I knew I'd get to hang out with him all day. When the divorce became final, an event that was foreshadowed by the sound of loud and often scary fights between my parents, I pretty much saw him less and less for the rest of my life. He came around and when he did it was good but for the most part he didn't come around. At the time I could not understand why since he lived pretty close to me even after the divorce. I mean "walking distance" close. There was only one period of time where he actually lived far away and by then the absence of his presence was already beginning to grow on me. He wasn't a bad dad. He was great when he was around. The problem was that he just wasn't around very much.

But you know who was there? My Mom. No excuses. Nothing else better to do, nothing more important than her kids. It clearly left an impression. My mother was at every sporting event, every concert and play, every important event of my life to the point of being like, "Mom, it's OK. You can sit this one out," But no! She wouldn't hear of it. She was and still is dedicated. If there was a way for her to be presen,t she would be there. I think when I realized that my dad was not giving the same effort as Mom, it was a bit devastating. This slow unraveling of character was like watching your favorite Disney character at the Magic Kingdom take off his fake head to get a breather from the Florida heat and smoke a cigarette. As you watch the truth unfold, you have a hard time processing that your hero is fallible and only a human inside.

I don't know if I ever thought he was completely perfect but what I'm referring to is the lens through which you look at your father through when you are a young boy growing up. You see him as the biggest, fastest and strongest man you know and, somehow by some luck-of-the-draw, he belongs to you! He can beat up any other dad on the block and he can take on any challenge. He can basically do anything. However, somewhere along the line, you realize none of these things are true and that fathers do not possess any of those superhero-like attributes in the first place. Your dad might be overweight, too skinny or too tall or too short. He might be bald or really hairy, way too affectionate or not affectionate at all. Maybe he seemed perfect on the outside. Maybe he had a perfect body, maybe he dressed and smelled perfect all the time but somewhere along the line, the truth came to the surface and showed you that though his exterior was shiny and fun to look at his interior couldn't have been further from perfect. So no, he wasn't perfect and now you know the truth if you didn't already. How I came to terms with my own set of truths would stand to shape the rest of my life.

Though the lights turned on in high school, I wasn't upset about it until college. It was time to go and start the rest of my life on my own and all of a sudden my dad wanted to have some kind of deep meaningful relationship with me while I was ready to head out the door. Why now? The thought had crossed my mind that because of my dad's age (he was then 58 approaching 59 years old) that he wanted to reconnect with all of his adult children because he could see his life passing by. Somehow he wanted to make amends for the time that was lost but I was 18 and college bound. Formative years were over. The chance to watch me discover the world was through. The opportunity to influence and shape a young man's life had passed. I had to "find myself" on my own now and as far as I was concerned there was no reason to start caring now when my life hadn't been his priority for all the previous years. After that, there wasn't much thought given to the subject accept on the rare occasion that I would come back into town or on a phone call I'd get as a check up. The awkward and void filled conversation would lead to something like "we need to talk…" and it would be the same old story about how he didn't understand why no one would call him or come and visit. I mean the audacity right? Why was he asking me about coming to see him? I had never been a priority to him so why would he be that to me now? I would placate him and move on.

    Then one semester in a psychology class, we were learning about human behavior, hierarchy of needs, family structures and roles and it hit me. There were so many things in my life that were tied to my dad. So many insecurities I had about being a young man that he could have addressed and so many questions left unanswered because of the lack of his presence in my life. Some things might not have been answerable but just the shear fact of knowing that I had access to the answer may have been enough. But I didn't. He wasn't there when I needed him. Sure, he was physically in front of me some of the time, but the investment wasn't made in the crucial stages and I was left with a mother doing her best to scrape by and raise a boy all by herself. Women are wonderful creatures equipped to do many things, but I believe only a man was meant to raise another man to reach his full potential and I think somewhere deep inside the heart of a mother she knows this is true. Mom did what she could and, by the grace of God, she did a great job with what she had but there was no replacing dad's God-given position and responsibility.

    After I graduated college, I moved back home and though now armed with this new education that made it easier to understand, I was still a little resentful. The next phase of my life was about to begin and I felt that as a Christian I had a decision to make. I could bury this part of my life down for the rest of my life and write it off as just the way the cards fell because "it really wasn't that bad" or I could address it head on so that it wouldn't be an issue hidden under layers of emotions that could potentially be a time bomb that would surely affect my life, my marriage, and my future children. The decision seemed clear but executing wouldn't be so much.

    How do you stand in front of a man who thinks he's done a good job fathering you and tell him that has not? In 1 Timothy 5:1 we see a strong direction on addressing a man who is older and over you:

> *"Do not rebuke an older man but encourage him as you would a father…"*

But this man is my father. This truth didn't make addressing the issues I had any easier. You see, through all of this, even though I was angry, even though I had a right to be angry, even though I couldn't remember my dad being at birthday's and Christmas', even though I couldn't remember my dad being at sporting events that I was involved in throughout all of my grade school years and even though this was the man that my mother had said caused her so much pain throughout the course of their relationship of 20 plus years, he was still my dad. There was and I believe always will be a soft spot in my heart for him. I knew I was loved I just didn't know why I wasn't prioritized and that's what I needed to get to the bottom of.

So we had the talk. The talk of all talks. The one I had been dreading for so long. I was going to lay into him. Really let him know how I felt about all these years and to a degree this is what happened. But what also happened was for the first time I got to hear his side of the story. What I found out about my dad that I never knew before was that in his eyes, he was doing a better job than he ever had shown to him. His father's idea of being a good dad was coming around every now and again and giving my dad some cash, then disappearing into thin air. And though my dad was a close second, I would say that the impression he left was definitely better than that. He was never short with affection or including me in what he saw fit and our Saturday time together seemed to me to be just as fun for him.

He didn't know what he was doing. He said to me " when you start this thing, nobody hands you manual on how to be a parent. You just do the best you can with what you got." How do you argue with that? There was a genuine look of confusion on his face as I berated him with the "facts" of my upbringing and the damage that was left in his "lack of fathering" aftermath. I told him about year after year of going to church on father's day in the absence of his presence and how the tears would roll down my face because the pastor would honor all the dad's in the room but mine was nowhere to be found. I told him about countless times I would look into the stands from a field of play, , searching for the approving eyes of the one man I could call my own, only to met with the on look of strangers who had no bearing in my life. One after another, I hit him with all the facts from my side of the fence because I was determined to get this done once and for all.

And then silence. Awkward, pain-filled, silence. As far as he was concerned he was a rock star dad. We spent several Saturdays together, we worked on cars, we watched movies together and all this through the years after my parents were divorced, so why would he not think he was better than his dad? Why wouldn't he believe that throughout the course of his parenting life he had done a great job and now in his golden years, when it was time to slow down spend some more time with his loving children, that they wouldn't be there?

It was like watching a ship sink. It was slow and painful and I could tell he was remorseful and a bit helpless. Then it occurred to me. How would I respond should the roles be reversed? How could I handle my son or daughter saying to me "dad, I know you did the best you knew how to do, but it wasn't good enough?" How would that make me feel? It's no wonder the writer in 1 Timothy says to "encourage" or "exhort" an older man. After having worked a lifetime at something, no one wants to hear "Hey dad. You sucked as a father. P.S., no one likes you."

He apologized; and though I didn't get the years back in that instance, it was enough. It was all I needed and all I could tangibly have at that moment. I had a choice to make at that point. Forgiveness is a tricky thing and it's funny how sometimes a show of remorse is really all we are looking for to deal it out. After that day, not much changed. I understood him a little better and the reasons why he did what he did and that made the decision to forgive him that much easier. In looking back on that moment now, I still think it was the best decision I could have made. My father has since passed away since finishing the writing of this book. He'll never get a chance to see it completed but I am OK with that because I said all I needed to say and chose to forgive. I chose to let it go and be better for my own sake, not his.

What about you? Many of you have never had the opportunity to have the conversation where you get to pour your heart out and have it received with a contrite heart. Some of you don't want to have the conversation because it hurts too much and for some its is physically impossible to do so, so what then? How do you move on from there? Well, what I didn't say earlier was that prior to me and my father's big conversation was that I had already decided to forgive him. In Matthew 6:14-15 Jesus makes a pretty strong case for forgiveness by saying:

> *"For if you forgive men their trespasses, your heavenly Father will also forgive you. But if you do not forgive men their trespasses, neither will your Father forgive your trespasses."*

My choice to forgive wasn't to show my dad that I was now OK with all that had happened in the past. Forgiveness was for me. After that psychology class, I had grown very angry. More angry about anything I had ever been upset about in my whole life. Like a growing cancer, its affect was spreading inside of me and all I could think about was how bad being angry made me feel. I hated it. I hated how it affected me. I knew there was no way out but to forgive and let it go even if it were to just move on in life. I didn't have a father figure but I did know that there were men out there that had similar situations and had lived it out well enough to tell about it. They had even managed to be better men and that's what I wanted. I wanted to be better because I had deserved better but even if I didn't get it, I was now determined to give "better" to someone else. But this journey would begin with forgiving him right then and right there. Freeing my dad of any mental debt I had added up against him would in turn free me up from being the person maintaining that debt. It meant that I didn't have to charge it against my kids or maintain the weight of it for the rest of my life either. But more than all of those things, I knew and still know how much Christ is still forgiving me on a daily basis. I couldn't hold this against him and expect my heart to be seen and prayers to be heard by my heavenly father.

In Matthew 18:21-35, the parable of the Unforgiving servant illustrates a king's servant being shown forgiveness of a debt owed. However this same servant that had been shown mercy turns around and does not show that same grace to someone who owed him a debt. When the King gets wind of this action, he then tortures the servant until the original debt is paid. It doesn't say how he paid his debt but the implication is that the "torture" could have very well been part of the payment. The takeaway here is that if you believe in Christ, and you carry His name as your own, you have been shown mercy. Your sins are taken away at the mere recognition of who He is. You cannot afford to hold onto debts owed you because you do not possess the funds to pay Christ back for what He has done for you. None of us do. It is the gift that none of us can repay. What we can do, what we are commanded to do, what we so desperately need to do, is show that same grace that we live in to those who have yet to see it for themselves. In doing so, we free them but more importantly we also free ourselves.

And so it was done. I told my dad I forgave him and that I still loved him and that the only way that forgiveness was even possible was because of Christ's love for us all. I agreed to spend more time with him under one condition. That was that we would move forward in our lives together; we would stop dwelling on the past, start fresh and create a new future and we did exactly that.

At that point my life's journey was headed across the country far from where I grew up and I knew what time I had left to be with my dad on a regular basis, was now short. We took the next year and a half and spent a lot of time together. This was some of the most precious time together with my dad that I can remember and I am so glad we had a chance to move forward. This single event catapulted me into the beginning of the rest of my life and I would say not only shapes the way I see fatherhood but in conjunction with the bible, would also stand to shape my view of manhood.

CHAPTER THREE
TIME TO MAN UP
TURN YOUR G.I. JANE INTO G.I. JOE

"Men are made to be pursuing something large epic, and lifelong. Men are made to be about something beyond just the immediate."
-Stephen Mansfield on a Family Life Today radio broadcast

So much of being the dad you want to be is locked up, first and foremost in being the man you need to be. We hear the term "man up" a lot these days. It's out there in society in all aspects of American culture but the concept is something that is globally understood. That being that there are unique traits that are only associated with manhood and if you are a real man, then you will possess these traits." What these traits actually are vary greatly amongst people groups but we could all probably agree on a few of them. A "real man" must make an effort to be brave and fight if necessary for those whom he loves, he must strive to be strong whether in a physical or a mental capacity and he must make a valiant effort in being able to provide for himself at least if not for his family in some capacity. Notice I didn't say anything about actually succeeding or accomplishing these traits nor the about age at which these things are accomplished. With the man who at least tries to do these things, society can muster up respect.

However if a man does not even try, then what kind of a "real man" is he? Stepping up to the plate is where the real challenge of fatherhood exist, not in the success of fatherhood. We don't praise our military because they win every war. We are proud of them because they exist! And it is because they exist that we have the opportunity to win wars in the first place.

WHAT DOES IT MEAN TO BE A MAN?

The implication of the term "man up" is pretty clear but why do we hear it so much? It seems to me if that there were enough men actually living up to the statement, that it would render itself useless. If enough men were living out the expectation of what being a man is then no one could say, "man up" cause there wouldn't be anything to compare the lack of manning up to.

The position of manhood comes with great responsibility. In fact, the majority of the properties associated with the title, infer a position of strength, wisdom, and honor. Superhero type stuff. These qualities are not that of riding on a horse and saving a princess, though at one time they may have been, but are the day to day type qualities that the unsung heroes wear proudly. These are the men that place others needs before themselves, men that honor their wives both when she is around and when she is not. Men that play with and make time for their kids and instill lifelong lessons in their teens. Men that pray for and seek God on behalf of there homes and all that they are responsible for. These are men that value the position of leader, as crucial and take it with the utmost seriousness. These are men that see all these mentioned things and keep trying to live it out though they continually fail at them. These are the men that are real. They are humble warriors; Men that don't start battles, but will finish them if need be.

How many "real men" can you count on your two hands? Men that possess these types of qualities? Not many I'd bet. Do you see these qualities in yourself? Why or why not? I can count a few but I think that's because I have been fortunate enough to be around men that seek after God whole-heartedly and pursue knowing who Jesus Christ is personally. Outside of these elite few, the crowds of "real men" who aren't afraid of "manning up" gets thinner and thinner. I see a lot of males around projecting what pop culture says is "manly", but not a lot of men. Let me say this, wanting to know God more does not make a boy into a man although it's a great start.

So what gives? Why is there such a lack of "real men" in the world today and why does it even matter? It matters because the attack on manhood is real! True masculinity is on the decline and is being shunned instead of being celebrated. The attack of masculinity is devastating and evident in many facets of life. Media, for example, has been portraying dads as bumbling idiots for years. From Married with Children to Modern Family, (Anyone else notice the Ed O'Neil pattern?) the characters are based on generalizations that says the father figure in homes is absent minded and or disengaged. Over time this characterization has gained traction in the real world and many men have just adopted this philosophy as their truth. So is art imitating life or is life imitating art. I'd say a little of both. The real life repercussions of men absolving themselves of their fatherhood roles have been devastating to societies perception of fatherhood. My brother-in-law told me once, that you can always get into any restaurant you want on Father's day without a wait. If you didn't get the inference, what he was saying was that fathers are so disregarded in society that you do not have the same problem you have on Mother's Day when trying to get into a restaurants. I couldn't help but laugh because he had a point. It's sad but true.

So is dad supposed to be a bumbling idiot? Or is he supposed to be the "go to guy" in clutch situations. Or in any situation for that matter? I think the answer is clear but there are so many men choosing the first option for the sake of convenience. The reality is that most men wouldn't even know that there is another option. Poor examples combined with poor execution has left our generation with a lot of confusion as to what exactly a real man even looks like and which definition is correct. It's a combination of circumstances that is crippling the male spirit and is being passed on to each proceeding generation. Every generation is left scrambling to define what real men are supposed to look like and with every generation that passes, we get further and further away from the truth.

Men today have traded their warrior spirits for passivity and convenience. Fatherlessness is only a symptom of greater issues that lie just below the surface of a man's heart. When uncovered, you find that fear, addiction, laziness and distraction run rampant. The attack on manhood is a substantial part of a greater picture though. There is a very real spiritual war going on where our soul's eternal destination is at stake and as a result, lives are literally hanging in the balance both in the physical and spiritual world.

I believe the attack on men is a critical piece to the destruction of the home. If you can take out a leader, his troops will scatter and similarly when men are displaced as leaders in their homes, chaos ensues. I am not implying that woman cannot do the job of running a home however if you talk to most woman who are actually running a home by themselves they would probably tell that they would welcome the help of a good man. You do not even have to be a Christian to see that the lack men in homes affects young boys and girls which in turn affects future generations. Our lack of understanding in the value of our position as men, allows a back door to be opened to the enemy. This lets him slip in from behind and do what he does best.

HE STEALS, KILLS AND DESTROYS...

One of the devil's many attacks on men has been directed at his confidence. If you can steal a man's prowess, then you can beat him into submission in turn making him do whatever you want him to do. If you can replace authentic manhood with perceived manhood you can change the trajectory of human history. If you can make a man feel less than he is in his mind then you can feed him lies that he'll believe and fight for as truth. The devil has been stealing our confidence for centuries. By doing this he knows that he undermines the God-given anointing we have as men to lead with strength. When men in this day and age see their leadership waning in the eyes of those who follow them, they have had a tendency to concede. We say, "Alright I give in. This is too hard" or "I don't want to be the bad guy so I'll go the easy route". When we do this we have fallen into the very trap that the devil wants. Satan knows that if he can under-mind the pillar-like strength of the man in a home, then it is very likely that that house will fall.

One of the greatest conduits by which the gospel of Jesus Christ has been shared through out the ages has been the central nucleus of the family. The enemy knows that if he can eliminate the family structure, then he can severely impact the power of the gospel throughout the world. But it doesn't start with the macro, it starts with the micro. The enemy is smart enough to not make his plans plain to see. It's not the large things like infidelity that destroy the home however it's the things that led up to the act that create the chaos. It starts with the subtle things like a man's mind and what he allows in it as well as whom he surrounds himself with. It starts when mom and kids don't learn about the character and nature of God through dad's daily example and are then are forced to find examples on their own, that is of course if they are even looking. Can you see how dangerous it becomes for a family if the man in their own home is not even attempting to be an example of Christ? If no example is given, no example will be followed.

We have to understand that when men can't stand straight and true, the weight that they are designed to carry in daily responsibilities, fall on those who were never meant to carry that weight. "Bearing the weight" of manhood is mostly referred to in the metaphorical sense. However isn't it funny that when you compare the biological structure of men to women,

men are typically larger, taller, stronger and heavier. Everything about a man in a physical sense is rigid and structured or designed to be a "weight bearer". Women are generally smaller, lighter and when compared to a man's physique, weaker. A woman's body is naturally built for nurturing, warmth, and comfort. From their scent to their body fat percentage, they are designed with care-giving in mind not to mention a whole host of other qualities that are unique to their gender. Though I am speaking in generalities and mainly referring only to the physical, you can plainly see that there is order to the unique designs of men and women, which is an indication of purpose.

When you can see how the Creator is setting life in motion and giving purpose to all things right down to the very function of cells and micro-organisms, you can also see how the role of men in the world has a distinct function and purpose and also why the attack on that purpose is so great. Men play a vital role. Adversely you can also see how when men do not show up for their role by buying into the lie that they don't matter, disorder soon follows.

If you can steal a man's confidence in who he is and what he is purposed for, then you have brought him to his knees and made him susceptible to a deathblow. I mean this both figuratively and literally. I have heard of and seen men brought to the point of breaking over and over again. Not because they were fighting so hard and were just growing weary but because they accepted defeat even before the battle begun.

In the parable of the talents found in Matthew 25:14-30 we see three men. All have been given a task to do which was to be a watch guard over the masters property. But the men were not given the same amount of responsibilities. They were given to according to certain conditions, those conditions were based on what unique skills each of them possessed as individuals.

"...to each (were given) according to his ability."

The first guy sees the task at hand and doubles the property that he had been given and since it was the most, in quantity, out of the three it's easy to say that he was probably the most gifted or talented in some way. He had the most resources to make doubling the property even possible. The next guy does the same thing. He didn't have as much as the first guy did and if we are hinging on the above verse, he wasn't as talented either but with what he did have he too also doubled in return. Now, what you see happen next is what so many men do. The last man in verse 24 says this:

> "Master, I knew you to be a hard man, reaping where you did not sow, and gathering where you scattered no seed, so I was afraid and I went and hid your talent in the ground. Here you have what is yours."

This guy let his fear of doing a bad job cripple him into doing no job at all. He hid the property in the ground. Man! If anyone ever needed a "hey dude, you need to man up!", it was this guy. This guy didn't even try because he was afraid of the responsibility and the person who gave him that job. If you keep reading, the master responds with this:

> "You knew that I reap where I have not sown and gather where I scattered no seed? Then you ought to have invested my money with the bankers, and at my coming I should have received what was my own with interest."

Has asks the servant a question and you can almost hear the sarcasm. "So you knew the type of man I am and you still did nothing?" Then if that wasn't bad enough, the master then schools the servant on how the very least he could have done would have been better than doing nothing at all. He says "you could have at least put it in a bank where it would have grown interest!" If you keep reading you'll see that the servant pays a severe price for his laziness and for giving into his fears.

Many men are no different. The irony of this story is that this type of mind set speaks against the very nature of who we are as men. Everything about a man's character says, "I want to be strong, stand firm, I want to give life and I want to show up and get stuff done!" But the thinking and doing of today's men are two different things. Far too often men are letting the voice of fear stand in the way and instead of at least doing something, we do absolutely nothing. This renders us completely ineffective. Ineffective at our jobs, our relationships and our purposes in life. By being ineffective we are robbed of the life giving effects we can have if we are willing to put the fear behind us, do the work and be who we are supposed to be. We are supposed to be strong. We are supposed to be firm. We are supposed to bring life to everything around us.

In order for a man to be a part of bringing life into the world, physically and biologically speaking, he must rise to the occasion and assert his position to the point of expelling seed. A limp man is only good for getting rid of waste. Are you picking up what I am laying down? I am picture painting again, only this time it's an anatomy diagram. Again, this is true in physical as well as the spiritual. If you look closely you will see the parallels God has built in to the physical world in order to give a glimpse and a clearer understanding of our spiritual nature and this is true in this case. Men were built to give and put out not take and receive. Everything in our nature both physically and spiritually speak to this truth. When we as men believe the opposite is true, order is disrupted. We can convince ourselves that our roles are not as such but then we have bought into the deception that has been laid out before us.

If Satan can rob the confidence of who you are as a man, then he can leave you vulnerable for the kill. If he can kill your purpose, he can destroy your legacy. By stealing and killing a man's purpose Satan is ensuring that the next generation of men fall into the same destructive pattern of apathy. This trap is working and has been working for generations. The pandemic of fatherless homes, in my opinion, starts way before a man fathers children and then decides to leave them. It starts when those men were boys and they didn't have fathers to learn from. Then those same boys, father their own generation without having learned the skills needed to be the fathers of that generation. One generation's failing fatherhood falls on the next and so the cycle continues and the gradual deteriorating of the Gospel fades with it.

So how do we make the cycle stop? The devil is in the business of messing things up. He rearranges order, causes confusion and wreaks havoc on all created things. At least for now, it appears that the scales have been grossly tipped in his favor. That's what he would like us to believe anyway. He would love for us to standby and not do anything because it seems like a hopeless cause. He would love for us to quit before we even start but in reality, the scales are not in his favor at all. The devil would have us believe that he is winning so that we would lose hope. However he is just cheating. The devil likes to keep his finger weighing down the sample pan. He's a cheater and a liar. He knows that if men can reach a glimpse of their potential or if they can scratch the surface of being affective in their sphere of influence, that the effect would be so great that it would not only change their own lives but everything around them! The good news is that this is true for you too. Buried deep inside of you is a man. A real man. A man's man. A man that has a great purpose and a man that will show up with whatever he has in his hands to do whatever he can because he knows that anything is better than nothing at all.

So many of the root problems that prevent men from being good dads is that they first don't know how to be good men. The reasons that this is true are many, however instead of focusing on why it's true we must focus on how to make it not true. Our best example of manhood and fatherhood is in the father of all fathers. The hero of all heroes. In Psalm 68:5 David writes about this hero and describes Him as the:

Father of the fatherless and protector of widows

> *is God in his holy habitation.*
> *God settles the solitary in a home;*

 This God has men like you and me in mind when he is watching out for those of us who didn't have a role model growing up and are now deeply affected by it. This verse literally says that God gives a purpose to those without purpose and He watches over those whom are weak and who have been cast out by society. If you take this to heart this is great news because if the God of the universe is on your side, it doesn't matter how small of man you think you are. It only matters how big of a man He thinks you are. If you are trusting in God for your very sustenance, then this promise is one you can build your manhood on. Your earthly father may have abandoned you but your heavenly father specializes in adopting and caring for the fatherless. Not only does he take orphans in, he trains them up and sends them out to do the same. Though you are weak, you can be made to stand strong. Through God's plan for your life you can shut the door behind you that may have been left open for you to fail. You can show up and bring life to everything your hands touch when you belong to the God who made men. When you decide to filter your life through God's order, you will begin to see the purpose He has set in place for the role of manhood. You will see how obtainable it is and how it's already in you waiting for you to take hold of it. You will also see the unique role God has for you to play in life and if you follow through with fear behind you, you will be a force to be reckoned with. When you are around, no one will ever have to tell you to "man up", because a real man will be present and apparent for the whole world to see.

CHAPTER FOUR
SAVE YOUR HEROINE IN DISTRESS
PRIORITIZING YOUR LEADING LADY

There is this epic scene that I feel like we have all seen in any superhero movie. It is that perilous moment where our hero has been put in a predicament that requires him to make an impossible decision. It usually involves our hero's love interest and goes something like this: Our hero, who has chased the villain to bring him to justice, has already overcome several obstacles and now finally has come face to face with his enemy only to find that the villain has gotten the drop on him. In the villain's possession is the one thing that our hero cares about the most, the girl. After a sarcastic monologue, where the villain outlines the obvious impossibility of the situation, he leaves our hero with a decision to make and usually not enough time to make it in. Save the girl or save the world. If he saves the girl, then there will be no world to live in with that girl. If he saves the world, then there will be no girl to live in the world with. Horrible, right? What should he do? The only thing a superhero must do, and that is save both! A horrible cliché that we have all seen a thousand times. But what would you do? Save the girl or save the world?

In the movie Spider-Man (2002 version) this scene occurs where Spider-Man and the Green Goblin are entangled in battle high up on a New York bridge. The Green Goblin has Mary Jane in one hand and in the other, dangling by a severed cable, is a sky car full of children and adults. Before Spider-Man has enough time to decide which he'll save first, the Green Goblin has dropped both. In any number of Superman movies or comics, Lois Lane is falling from a building, falling from a helicopter or falling through space in an escape pod (seems like she is always falling from somewhere. I mean can a hero get a break!?) and Superman has to come in and save the day. Good thing he is always close enough or fast enough to make that save.

In the same way, as husbands and fathers, we are juggling a ton of decisions that need to be made every day, decisions that require us to swoop in and save the day. In our quest for heroism we understand the expectation of us to solve problems and provide. We understand that we are looked to for strength, guidance and wisdom even if we don't have it. The big things are clear to us; it is the nuances that are a bit more elusive. It is the subtle things that we tend to miss, when really it is the collective efforts of these subtle things that can add up over time to support us in our efforts of being the hero we really want to be. Because being the hero means we are in charge and in control. It means we are the one guy your family can rely on to get the job done no matter how big or small. But you know what? It's not just the hero, it's the SUPERhero. Superheroes nail the nuance. Super heroes are dedicated to the details. Becoming a superhero is the art form we have to master.

SAVE THE GIRL, SAVE THE WORLD

The first key to all of this lies in winning your leading lady's heart and keeping it won on a daily basis. Impossible, right? It definitely might feel that way at times. In fact, I believe that most men give up after a short while because women have a tendency to be moving targets. Men don't really like moving targets. It makes conquering that much harder and when it comes to conquering, easy is good. We don't like to play games where the rules change in the middle of playing the game. Many Madden football games come to mind where friends end up in arguments 'cause the rules change in the middle of a play. That type of game is illogical to a man's mind. To men, chaos in any endeavor is equal to war and in war there are no rules. So if you are playing a game that has no rules then you have accepted that there will be casualties and one of those casualties might be you. Attractive, right? Not really. That's one of the many reasons why so many young men hesitate in stepping up to the plate of marriage. They fear marriage will take them out, proverbially speaking of course, but sometimes literally as well. Out of fear of the unknown and the ever-changing female rule book, young men say things like, "Well, I can see that marriage is a big responsibility that is going to require a lot of me, most of which I don't already have to offer nor do I desire to offer up, so I think I'll wait till I have my life, money and/or job in order." We do this partly out of our desire to be noble and partly out of our desire to be responsible, but mainly out of our fear of failure. If the rules of engagement are constantly changing, the target is always moving, variables like bills, in-laws, and staying employed are randomly being thrown in the mix, in addition to not having proper examples that have successfully navigated those same waters, it is no wonder that the perception of young men is that it's better to get married only when there are no other options left. Then, if they do get married, they blindly fumble their way through it till it either kills them or someone in the couple calls it quits.

So a young man might decide in his head early on that he's never going to get married. Having to prioritize someone else all the time just doesn't sound that appealing. But then, one day, we get a little lonely and we get to thinking about our future. Since we can't ever really get away from how beautifully made God's daughters are, we start to play with the idea of marriage and that it might not be as scary if we take it a day at a time. So we dabble around with the idea of having a leading lady in our lives. Most modern men prolong or don't want that kind of responsibility for long as possible but let's say we do want to play the game of love with a woman.

In an ideal world, we would get to know everything we need to know up front before we play. But that's not how it works is it? Even in those who pre-screen their potential mates by living together, having sex, having babies, and doing life together in every capacity before ever seriously committing to each other and getting married find that the challenges of marriage are difficult. Because even if you think you have her figured out, once you throw all the variables of life into the mix, there really is no way for you to possibly know what to expect. So we deny, deny, deny. We deny our desire to be with woman in a permanent capacity out of fear of commitment and what that means. We deny the responsibilities of taking care of a family in exchange for companionship and love because it's too uncertain and expensive. We deny our God-given leadership ability by denying the responsibilities God has placed in front of us and, as men, we have suffered a devastating blow because of it.

Absolving our place as men leading in our homes has had innumerable effects on every sphere of life but especially in one place in particular. It has affected the heart of women. Somewhere deep inside the heart of a woman is a desire to be partnered up with hero, a knight in shining armor, a prince who saves her from a wicked witch and fire-breathing dragon. What they actually get more often than not, is a bum—a douche bag in stinky gym clothes who couldn't care less about saving her from a garden snake much less a fire-breathing dragon and they have become disappointed, angry and vocal about it. Yet we have the audacity to wonder why they don't respond to us sexually. We demand respect yet we give none in return.

Gentlemen, the onus to initiate any and all things in your relationship lies with you. You are the beginning and the end of all the issues in your home. Not because you are a male, remember you had nothing to do with that. You just got here like that. However, these are the responsibilities that are synonymous with the title of manhood and these are also the tasks of a father. Her responsibilities are different. Neither is better than the other, they are only different. Abandoning your position as the man in your home does not get rid of the responsibilities that come with that title. Those responsibilities will continue to exist whether you own them or not. They will continue to exist whether she takes over them or not and they will continue to exist whether your children decide to accept them for themselves one day or not.

Newsflash, gentlemen: If we do not prioritize loving our wives appropriately, *"appropriately"* being the operative word, then we have failed in our first duty to our family and cannot logically, in turn, expect there to be much victory in the pursuit of greatness in our home. This is something that is near and dear to the heart of God, so much so that in 1 Peter 3:7 (AMP) the Bible speaks directly to married men, saying:

> *...you married men should live considerately with [your wives], with an intelligent recognition [of the marriage relation], honoring the woman as [physically] the weaker, but [realizing that you] are joint heirs of the grace (God's unmerited favor) of life, in order that your prayers may not be hindered and cut off. [Otherwise you cannot pray effectively.]*

So basically God says that He can't even hear what you are saying to Him if you are not living with your wife in a way that exemplifies cognitive consideration, understanding and patience to the best of your ability. That's a pretty big deal considering the fact that, as Christian men, we should recognize that we cannot live this life on our own strength or merits so trying to do it without the help of the Almighty is insanity. I mean "ALMIGHTY" is His title, doesn't that say everything right there? Yet this is what we do when we live in a disorderly manner with our wives. We not only destroy our position in her eyes, we also block the communication lanes we have with God, leaving ourselves quite literally alone and on our own in life.

WHEN A MAN LOVES A WOMAN

So first thing's first; get on board with doing right by your wife. If there is anything that is dividing the two of you, find out what it is and eliminate it. It doesn't matter who is wrong and who is right. Do you want to be right or do you want to be married? Do you want to be a hero or do you want to be a douchey bum? Initiate the conversation and do it often. By doing so you'll show her that you are in pursuit of her affections. If there is a lot of damage, don't expect this to work overnight. It may have taken you a long time to get where you are so don't expect healing to happen overnight. Don't wait for her to come to you. You go to her. Set up a time and place and make it official if need be. Do it with no expectation of anything in return from her but make sure she can hear you out. Admit that you have failed her as a husband, a leader, a provider or whatever shoe fits. Bear the weight of the wrong because your shoulders are designed for it and because you desperately need her in your corner, then go and actually make the changes. All the talk will not mean much if she cannot immediately and tangibly see the changes being made with consistency. Then give her all the time she needs to heal and restore trust.

The weight of the Roman cross (a 100 lbs. if just the crossbeam but up to 300 lbs. if it was an entire cross) on Christ's emaciated bare back probably didn't feel any better than this conversation but somehow I don't think your situation is as extreme as his was. It might feel like it emotionally because of the baggage that can easily accumulate through the years. Burdens and resentment can build up but if the same spirit that raised Christ from the dead lives in you, then you'll be able to make through any tough conversations you need to have or any amount of time you need to heal. Don't be afraid to get help either. Bringing in a coach is not a sign of weakness but a sign of great strength and determination. A word of caution on getting counsel. I suggest that you only seek advice from like-minded individuals. Gaining wisdom from people who do not have the same worldview as you is like going to the dentist when you need a cardiologist. They both look the same but their specialties are very different. Getting mentors who either have a Christian marriage you want to model yours after or a degree in counseling with a Christian world-view would be the only help from other people I would recommend getting, depending on the severity of help you may need.

A relationship with Christ is the center from which everything on the home front flows in a proper order. The very next relationship that is of the utmost importance in a father's life is the one he has with his wife. No effective anointing will be had by a father to reach his children if the relationship to their mother is out-of-order. The views your kids hold of you and of God will often and directly correlate to how you emotionally and spiritually connect with your wife. The Bible parallels the relationship of man and woman to Christ and his bride. His love for her is physically and spiritually sacrificial and is consistent and unending. This is the same example we need to live out in our homes. It's not easy but it is worth it.

One amazing strength that men have when they are living to their potential is to see a challenge, accept it, and go full force at it. A man will relentlessly pursue the goal in front of him, almost to his detriment if he deems the challenge worthy of his time and effort. It could be a 12 hour work day or 12 hour video game session. When something has engaged our minds, our hearts follow. This is even truer when the engagement involves a physical element. This is why we can easily lose ourselves in hours of physical activity, be it on a basketball court or viewing sexually stimulating material on-line. There is a strong connection that men have to physicality even if it doesn't always play out in a physical way. You can be an introvert, a bookworm or an intellectual and an academic. It doesn't matter. The gratification that you get from being alone, reading a good book, or exploring new topics of study results in a physical response. It just plain feels good. There is a personal reward. So why not approach the exploration of your wife in the same way? Knowing that, in the end, if we do not grow weary, we too will benefit.

Instead of viewing the changes as a moving target, view them as a variable that keeps the game interesting. An audible if you will. In football a good quarterback reads the defense and, based on the environment, makes changes to keep advancing the ball. Your wife's change in behavior may be a result of many things affecting her environment so her "audibles" could be a way to keep her game in play. As with the other ventures we put our mind to in order to receive a reward of some kind, there will be rewards in doing this with your wife. It might not always result in sex. Sometimes it might result in a deepening of your relationship that could far outlast your years to have sex. However it could result in sex! It's a win, win! We do this in many other areas of our lives throughout our lives. We do it with our careers, with sports and with our friends. So why should it be any different with our wives? Instead of looking at her like a moving target that is impossible to please, trying viewing her as a challenge to be conquered. Your relationship with her is a game to be learned, practiced and mastered, but not in the sense that says, "I own you. You are mine!" However in the sense that says, "I know you, I see you. You are familiar to me and it is my pleasure to be yours."

Sure, some of the rules are going to change over time but can you honestly say that you are the same person you were 10 years ago? If you have kids, try to imagine pushing out of your body something the size of a watermelon only it's coming out of something the size of lemon and see if that doesn't change you at the very least in a physical sense. Or, if she was like my wife and had a C-section (three of them), imagine having a flesh wound positioned on your body so that the weight of your entrails literally sits against the wound so that when you stand up, you run the risk of your guts falling out. I forgot to mention that the wound looks like you got in a sword fight with a gladiator and lost. This cut is required to be held together with steel staples not only on the outside but on the inside as well. Sound fun? Not really. Think about these things and things like them when she doesn't feel sexy as a result of having a baby and figure out a way to restore her confidence, not only in herself but in the love that you have for her, because this is what she had to go through to allow you the title of "Father".

Maybe you are well beyond the years of having babies. Maybe you have been together for a long time or sometime longer than a few years. Think of all the times she has had to put up with you and remember she could have been with someone else but she chose you just as much as you chose her. You do not have to really dig too far to find a reason, but if you need one, think about it and then get to action. If we can apply ourselves to things that have no eternal value, like careers, sports, or video games then we can surely make an effort to prioritize and invest in the one relationship that is meant to last us till we see the one whom relationships are meant to be modeled after.

WITH GREAT POWER, COMES GREAT RESPONSIBILITY

By prioritizing your wife, you are in a position of power. When Jesus faced Pilate to be crucified, Pilate said to him, "Don't you know that I have the power to crucify you or to set you free?" Jesus shut his argument down by reminding Pilate, "You would have no authority over me had it not been given to you..." The take away here is that the person who gives priority is the one with the power. No one took the life of Christ. He gave it freely. No one had power over him. He offered himself up. In the same way we show an incredible amount of strength and power in our position of husband and father when we give the priority to our wives.

In the movie Spider-Man, Uncle Ben reminds Peter Parker that, "With great power, comes great responsibility." Later I'll discuss this idea a bit further but for now, if we want to have great power, if we want to give great power to those around us beginning with our wives, then we must prioritize her heart and her needs even before ourselves. Only then can we move forward in the pursuits that God has for us wholeheartedly because only then will God hear our call. So if I were Spider-Man the trolley full of people wouldn't have had a chance because the no-brainer was Mary Jane. Sorry, kids.

CHAPTER FIVE
KEEP YOUR LEGACY INTACT
LET THE FORCE BE STRONG IN YOU.

Let me tell you the story of a particular hunter who found himself in a unique situation. The woods were unusually hot this particular morning and the air was thick with moisture, so much so that visibility had been slightly impaired because of the humidity in the air. Sweat beads dripped down his forehead into his eyes though the hunter refused to flinch. His focus was laser sharp and the only thing distracting him was the rumbling in his belly that started as a distant call but was now a loud, echoing siren that he was finding hard to ignore. He had a point to prove, not only to his prey but to himself. The point being that he was a lord over all the creatures in his domain. He had been given dominion over creeping and crawling things, especially with the purpose of providing for his family and tribe. The object of his trip would lie in waste if he failed to bring home spoils of some kind. Blinking in an inopportune moment would not only be seen as a sign of weakness but could potentially make him miss a chance at his target. Missing would be unacceptable. The weight of the survival of his people rested on his shoulders. The meat he brought home from a hunt like this made provision for many people, for a long time. It was not sport to him. It was life or death.

Ugh! But the nagging hunger in his stomach. The grumbling grew louder and more frequent. He had been putting it off for a while now but it was so persistent in reminding the hunter that it hadn't gone away and did not plan to until something was done about it. In the beginning he was resolute in ignoring it but the temptation was so constant and so frequent that giving in was starting to seem like a better alternative. He tried his best to focus on the task at hand, even bringing small snacks to help tide him over, but nothing was working.

It had been a few days since the hunter had been home even though home was not even very far away. He'd had no success to speak of so giving in now would mean he would have to start all over again. He would have to prep and repack all of his provisions, a task that could potentially take several days time. He would have to re-track any animal whose trail he was on, another task that could be potentially time consuming. The time, energy and resources he had invested in his current quest would go to waste. Not to mention the people he would have to face when he got back to camp. He would have to answer to the people who relied on him for strength and provision. He remained quiet though a mental war raged inside of him.

Maybe there was a way out though. Maybe if he could sneak away for a small meal, just enough to keep his mind sharp and to silence the hunger in his stomach, it would be enough. He would lose a day or so of tracking but if he died of hunger then none of it was worth it anyways. He wasn't that far from camp and he thought he saw some game closer to home on his way into this part of the woods. It might just be worth a shot. Some soup would do it. Yeah, a bowl of soup and maybe a piece of bread, he thought to himself, just enough to get me by this one time, then I'll just make sure I pack enough for the next time. A bowl of soup would be enough to hold him over and, at the very least, give him the immediate focus he needed to finish strong. Besides, no one would even care because every hunter he knew had been in a similar situation. If he just made sure to get it right the next time, he would be OK. Also, there was plenty of food at camp and this trip was just intended to stock up reserves. "I'll be fine," he said. Before he knew it, the Hunter had thought of more reasons to go back than to stay hunting. So he gave in.

As he reached the outskirts of camp his senses became heightened; the product of fasting for the last few days. He suddenly became keenly aware of the smell of food in the air. His mouth watered though his head was pounding with every step. Every muscle ached as he dragged his tired, sweaty and smelly body to his tent. He was sleep deprived and frustrated at his brief moment of weakness but he thought if he didn't waste any time at camp then he would be able to get right back out there to pick up where he left off. Frustration gave way to irritation so he picked up his pace. Closing in fast on his tent, he realized that the most amazing smell of cooking food was coming from none other than his own tent! His brother, known for being a pretty good cook, already had some food cooking. This is going to work out better than I could have even planned it, the hunter thought to himself. The food is already made! I'll just grab a bite and then head back out.

Famished, the hunter threw his weary body down and barked at his brother, "Hey, give me some of that and hurry up! I have to get back out to hunt." His brother, whose manners were a little more agreeable, responded with a proposition. "Give me your birthright, and I'll give you a bowl of my stew." WHAT? Did the hunter hear right? Brother is clearly joking. There is no way he is serious. The hunter responded, "I really don't have time for games, little brother." But there were no games being played and his brother quickly replied, "How badly do you want to eat? Trade me your birthright." Like a quick left to the jaw! The audacity! I mean, it wasn't even a fair trade.

The "birthright" of the two brothers' culture was an endowment that was promised to the firstborn son, in this case the hunter. It was basically a promised inheritance that was double of anything anyone else would get in the family. It not only promised material wealth but also the gift of divine favor that pretty much guaranteed the success of all that you put your hands to, whether it be work or family related. It was the promise of blessings to your children's children and it was a HUGE deal in this culture. It was the type of deal you don't joke about over a bowl of soup. How could the younger brother possibly think this was a fair trade never mind have the gall to even bring it up as a serious proposition? The hunter was infuriated. The combination of the absurdity of the request and the physical ailments that were running through his body had his emotions and cognitive decision-making skills severely impaired and his temper was running wild.

Wait a minute. This had to be a joke. His brother couldn't be serious. There was no way. The younger brother knew the implications of what he was asking for. He knew how absurd it sounded and knew that the trade was unfair. The hunter was totally being punk'd. Anger gave way to humor. The tension eased as the hunter started to laugh. "Sure, brother, whatever you want. After all, what good is my birthright if I die of starvation?"

Does this story sound familiar? Jacob and Esau, right? If you don't know it, it is a story found in the book of Genesis 25:27-34. If you do know it you'll remember that, in less than ten verses, a key plot point plays out in the drama that is these two brothers' relationship and if you blink you can miss the significance of it. After some time passes the selling of Esau's birthright would come back to bite him. Jacob would later come to collect on Esau's promise to transfer his inheritance. When Esau finds out what his brother has done, he vows to kill him. Can you blame him? But isn't it kind of his own fault? Esau was manipulated. To make matters even worse, you come to find out that his mother was in on the sabotage. But is it really anyone else's fault other than Esau's? He traded his position of "firstborn", something that he should have not even entertained, for a bowl of stew. In jest or in seriousness it was not something to be taken lightly. Esau traded something eternal for something temporal. The trade was rigged from the start and Esau didn't even know his destiny was being tampered with. His future was being determined by the decisions he was making and it didn't even matter that he was unaware. It is a scary thought to think that the same applies for us men when we play this dangerous game with our birthright. The stage was set and the stakes were raised for Esau and, given the right combination of circumstances, we have the ability to do the same thing.

According to the Bible, men were created first. This position endows us with certain responsibilities and, to some degree, certain rights. As "firstborn" we have an anointing that is different from that of women. We have been gifted physically, spiritually and emotionally in certain capacities that are completely different from that of a woman. These distinctions have purpose in the structure of the home, the order of the world and the hierarchy of the Kingdom of God and if we don't live them out then the order of these three institutions operates out of line.

There is a war being waged against us for our birthright but there can be no war where there are no soldiers willing to fight, only complete domination. Not having anyone there to fight does not change the existence of the enemy. If a man is handing over his birthright then he has handed over his promise for a future and if a man has no future to live for then he will only live for *the now*. When a man only lives for now, his concern becomes what makes him immediately happy or makes him feel good right now in the moment and not what is good for the long term.

THE HUNGER GAME

We are in an age that struggles deeply with addiction and not in the sense that we are used to hearing about. We are addicted to the drug called "feelings". Our way of life thrives on creating an environment that puts how we feel at the center of our decision making. The appetite for the way we "feel" is insatiable and if we are not "feeling" it, then it must not be for us. Our generation has a tendency to let our "feelings" dictate our actions no matter what the consequences, and why not? After all, how we *feel* is the only thing that matters. Who cares about the lives that are affected by our decisions? As long as we make sure we feel happy that is the only thing that matters. In fact, "feeling" like a man is actually more important to our generation than actually doing the things necessary to earn us the title. It is the same mentality that says, "If I can have sex with several women, or men, then I feel like I am the man; and since pop culture and the media says the same, then I can't be wrong. Besides, if I can't, it doesn't matter, 'cause I can just get sex on my computer or my phone so I actually don't need anyone else to make me feel like a man. I'll just do it myself." Or it says things like, "If I can make boat loads of cash, then I am a real man. It doesn't matter if I'm dishonest in how I achieve it; as long as I have it or at least can make it look like I have it then, again, I am the man. If I have more toys than anyone else, the latest clothes, cars or technology, then I am a real man. Even if I don't have those things, if I can make it appear as though I do, then I can portray the idea that I am, in fact, a "real man". And even though I am not a real man, it doesn't matter because as long as I *feel* like I am doing the right thing, that is actually more important than actually doing the right thing."

But it's all lies. The addiction to feeling like we are something has led us to being absolutely nothing in the long run. It has given the world many males but not enough men. In the moment, Esau's "feelings" of hunger overrode his ability to see that the trade was not even an equal one. By temporarily feeding his physical hunger pangs, he gave up his spiritual rights and his future promise. There was a moment of reasoning where he weighed the cost but because of his condition he did not make the correct choice.

OUR MODERN DAY SOUP

The forfeiting of our God-given birthright has given way to a false sense of security in temporal things that aim only to appease our flesh-driven nature. Pornography is a great example of this. Pornography has the power to alter our biophysical chemistry with the chemical release of dopamine in our brains. This chemical release in the brain leads us to believe that porn is a viable source of sexual and emotional satisfaction in our lives. However, it is not. It is a bowl of soup and I would say for the Superman that you are trying to be, it will be your kryptonite. Some of the greatest men in the Bible struggled with sexual temptation. Do not think you are the exception.

Pornography is one of those things that is an elusive killer because it works with your body's design. In 1 Corinthians 6:18, Paul writes about how sexual sin affects you in a way that is unique because all other sin is outside of your body, but sexual sin is against your body. I like to think of it as all other sin originates from the outside and makes its way in, whereas sexual sin is just the opposite. It originates from within our natural sexual desire and then moves outward toward action and becomes a physical manifestation. This eventually brings spiritual death (James 1:15). It's not like external drugs that can alter your body's chemical balance to the point where it can kill you, at least in the physical sense. It will, however, create in your brain chemical dependencies that are several times more addictive than cocaine. Pornography also doesn't trigger the brain's natural aversion system. That is the part of the brain that say's, "OK I'm good, I'm full," or "I have had enough." You can literally sit for hours and watch video after video giving you a virtual I.V. stream of stimulus that is altering how you think and behave. Still think it's harmless? William Struthers, a professor of psychology at Wheaton College, say's it like this:

> "The psychological, behavioral, and emotional habits that form our sexual character will be based on the decisions we make, whenever the sequence of arousal and response is activated, it forms a neurological memory that will influence future processing and response to sexual cues. As this pathway becomes activated and traveled, it becomes a preferred route--a mental journey--that is regularly trod. The consequences of this are far-reaching."

Trading our God-given anointing, influence and position for a temporal physical fix is a symptom of a deeply spiritual problem. We have traded the eternal blessings of marital sex for the temporal gratification of "make believe" self-sex because one is easier to obtain than the other—because the real thing with a real woman is a really hard thing to maintain but passing sex, non-emotional sex with a real person or with a computer, is quick, fast and mostly painless. But, again, the temporal satisfaction of a bowl of soup is only that; temporal. It holds you over until your appetite to feast rises up again. The problem is that now in our mind we have made up a fake source from which we can draw. A shallow well of "good feelings" that will placate our needs when the rest of life becomes too hard but, just like junk foods, pornography is a calorie dense food with zero nutritional value. It makes you spiritually fat, weak and lazy. It tastes good in your mouth but looks bad on your gut. It's easy to take in but hard to work off. The best remedy is to never have ingested it in the first place.

Pornography has a hold on this generation of men and boys like never before, mainly because of its accessibility. You used to have to go into a store and buy it but now with the press of a few buttons you can have it wherever you are. It has even permeated the hearts of women and young girls, altering their views of their own sexuality, romance and love. This attack is perpetual and redundant and its only aim is to destroy our God given destinies. If it doesn't take us out completely, it will severely alter how we get to our destination. There are countless men in the world, many of whom hold full-time ministry roles that are trading their birthrights for this type of soup. The attack is evident and clear. It is fiercely divisive because it uses our own design against us.

This particular area is one that is near and dear to my heart. My first exposure to pornography was at an early age. I want to say it was somewhere between 7 and 10 years of age. I remember seeing my dad place something above a cupboard in my house. I didn't know what it was he had put up there, but I saw him do it and curiosity took over. He was acting a bit suspicious and I was inquisitive. It was a recipe for disaster. I asked him what it was and, nonchalantly, he showed me a few pages. He said, "Oh, it's nothing, it's just pictures of girls, showing their (insert expletive here)." He meant nothing by it I'm sure. He probably thought at the right time it would probably even be good for me as a young man. What he probably didn't know was that I would never forget that moment. I would never forget what he said to me and those images would be burned into my head for a very long time. He didn't know that he had inadvertently kicked open the door to a struggle that would follow me for the rest of my life. It would affect my relationships, my view of myself and my view of the opposite sex. It would affect my relationships with girlfriends before marriage and it would also affect my relationship with my wife. I don't blame him, one, because I forgave him for all of that, and two, because I am sure that, with the way technology has advanced, this struggle would have come up regardless.

If God has a plan for your life it's probably not a stretch to think that the enemy has a plan for it as well. The enemy's plan is to steer you in a direction that is away from your destiny. Before I could even know that I had a purpose in God's eyes, the enemy had tried to set a hook deep in my mouth and I would argue that he was relatively successful. For many years after that, I traded my birthright for snacks, meals and full-on feasts, at times, of fleshy soup. Each time leading to a desire for more and each time driving a deeper wedge between me and my relationship with God.

It was not until many years later, my adult years, when I realized that I wasn't the only one struggling with this same type of addiction. Only then would I feel comfortable enough to reach out and get help through various resources. In fact, the issue has taken such a turn in today's society that what once was something shameful has turned into being something that pop culture has made humorous. "Oh, everyone looks at porn," "It's natural, it's normal" are the messages being pushed today and young people are drinking it down by the gallon. Now with social acceptance, ease of access, and a self-centered, narcissistic generation prevalent in the world today, the addiction of pornography is not even considered serious even though it is secretly devastating men, women and families across the globe.

These things are not surprising to hear when there is either a weak understanding of the purpose that God has for our lives or a deficit of knowledge in what the Bible has to say about these things. When a person has no idea of their value or purpose they will see no reason to invest in their eternity, which means they will only live for the moment. Therefore, if it feels good now, they will indulge themselves free of any concern for their future. It is not hard to see what buying into the lie of "trade me your birthright for this bowl of soup" is doing to the world and our future.

Pornography is only one example of this truth. Take out "pornography" and replace it with whatever your fix is and the truth still remains that if you trade your birthright, your God given purpose, your destiny of influence for X, you are giving up much more than you can ever imagine for a trade that isn't even remotely close to being worth it. Most of the time you will not even be able to see what you are actually trading it for, however it will never be an equal trade.

CHAPTER SIX
REACH BACK AND PASS FORWARD
YOU HAVE MUCH TO LEARN GRASSHOPPER, YOU ALSO HAVE MUCH TO GIVE.

There is a group of guys I know from a time long ago. These guys were your average guys from around the way. They had families and jobs. Some were probably well educated and some were average students. Most of them just took up a trade of some kind to make ends meet. Some were the highly regarded in their respective communities and most were just hard-working, blue-collar types. Some were younger and some were older; some were gifted with intellect and others were gifted in physical strength. Just everyday guys. If they were in today's day and age, they would probably range from academic enthusiasts and politicians to football-loving construction workers and electricians. These guys were, as one writer calls them, "remarkably unremarkable."

One day, while going about their normal everyday lives, each of them were approached and propositioned to drop what they were currently doing to pursue something that they had never done before. It would eventually cost each of them their lives, though at the time they didn't know it, but somehow the mystery seemed worth it. There would be no way for them to know how it would all turn out but if they placed their trust in this man named Jesus, it would promise to be an adventure nonetheless. Each of them had a decision to make. Internally examining and assessing their own need for something greater than themselves is a personal conversation that for some probably took place in a split second and for others took a little while to process. Either way, each man had to recognize his own need for something greater than what he already possessed and answer the call.

THERE COMES A TIME IN EVERY HERO'S JOURNEY WHERE HE MUST DECIDE.

This moment was the disciples' defining moment. Jesus was a controversial figure to align themselves with for a few reasons. He was from a small town called Bethlehem, whose claim to fame was the great King David, a king known for his tremendous abilities in battle and the favor God had on his life. This was significant because Jewish prophesy and scripture claimed that the Messiah that the Jews had been waiting for would come from Bethlehem and would also come from the line of King David. The word "Messiah" literally means "anointed" or "anointed one". It is used in a variety of settings to distinguish people of divine significance in the ancient world. This particular usage of the term in Jewish culture refers to a man whose destiny it was to be the savior of the Jewish people from political oppression. If the claims were true about Jesus that would mean he was also the manifestation of God in the flesh, however not just any god, but the God of their ancestors whose reputation amongst the Jews was legendary.

The Jewish people were originally a nomadic group with no country to call their own. Throughout the history of their existence they have been continually oppressed by political factions and regimes even to this day. At the time of Jesus' arrival, the Roman Empire was in control of the provinces in the Mediterranean region. If Jesus' lofty claims were unfounded then surely he would be facing extradition from not only the Roman government for claiming to be higher than Caesar, but from his own people as well for committing blasphemy against the Hebrew God. For the disciples to align themselves with Jesus meant that any persecution he would face would also be theirs to bear as well. A decision to follow this man meant that the disciples' lives would never look the same again. To their friends and family, following Christ probably looked as crazy as it sounded. So for each of them, the decision to follow him was extremely significant.

SOMETIMES YOU GOTTA TO DO, WHAT YOU GOTTA DO

There is a point in every person's life when you realize that you are simply better when you have help, that there is strength in numbers and tough situations are better when there are more people around to absorb the blow. I believe that in spite of all the opposition the disciples probably felt, this is why they chose to follow Christ. It was a deep seeded recognition that they needed his help. It is unfortunate that many men and fathers alike gravitate towards doing this life alone though what you will find is that they don't last very long on their own. Sure, for a time you can survive fatherhood and manhood on your own, never utilizing help from the seasoned veterans around you or acquiring the resources you need to be successful, but are you the type who wants to *survive* or would you rather *thrive*? I think for each of these men, the proposition of following Christ was a chance to thrive in a way that they had not been able to previously achieve on their own. It would surely mean a particular level of uncertainty but there would be adventure and opportunity that was greater than what they were each respectively doing at the time of the call. And though those things were great I don't think that is why they chose to follow Christ. I think that ultimately, each of them could not deny what they felt inside of their hearts when they would listen to Jesus speak. It was a chance to be more than just ordinary men. It was a chance to be epic. Christ's challenge to them was so impactful that they dedicated their lives to pursuing it completely.

Each man had to make a decision to reach back for the help he needed to move forward. They had to find something outside of themselves to help propel their own lives onward. Do you know anyone like that? Anyone who interests you so much that you would drop everything you are currently doing to be near them all the time? I can't really think of anyone in the flesh who would convince me to trade my job, family and the life that I have worked so hard to attain for such uncertainty. There are a handful of people who I would love to spend some time with to pick their brain because I find their life's path so interesting, like some world leaders whose schedule I would love to share for a day. There are a few others I would like to have a "not-so-close" encounter with, more like a "fly on the wall" sort of thing just observe how and why they make the decisions they make. When I think about this tier a few celebrities whose lives seem interesting enough to follow come to mind. There are even a few people in history that I would have loved to interact with on some level but maybe even fewer people whose life I'd like to be a part of. However, there is not one person, even in these categories that I would be willing to drop my whole life for just to follow. But for the disciples there was something about Jesus that was different and the result of their decision to follow him was enormous. It was so huge in fact, that you could say that every Christian church that has been established since these guys lived is a result of their decisions. You could easily say that every person in every age in every part of the world who has heard of or believed in the name of Jesus from then until now is the result of their decisions. Amazing to think about, right?

GETTING HELP ALLOWS YOU TO GIVE HELP

When the disciples reached beyond their own ability and looked for help in life, it positioned them to be able to give others the opportunity to do the same. Standing on the shoulders of someone stronger than themselves moved them to the next level and, eventually, the impact that it had on them as individuals would shape human history for the next two thousand years. Where do you need to do the same to affect your sphere of influence? Where do you need help in your life as a man and as a father and where can you go to get it? Whose shoulders can you stand on to move up? Who can you lock arms with in order to strengthen your position as man and a father in your home so that your legacy is strong and your children build on the foundation of strength that you have laid?

IT'S SO EASY A GIRL CAN DO IT

There is an amazing story of a young track and field athlete at an Ohio championship meet. In 2012, Meghan Vogal was competing in a few events over the course of back to back weekend meets. In the first weekend, she clenched a contending position at the state championship by passing two other runners in the last leg of a 4x800 relay. At the actual state championships the following weekend, she ran a 1600 meter race earlier in the day and won the race with a personal best time of 4 minutes, 58.31 seconds. After the awards and spending some time with family and friends she had only about an hour to prepare for the following meet, which was a grueling 3200 meter run. Any athlete knows that, after having trained, competed, trained, and then competed again, this would have been a difficult race to run, let alone win.

Early on in the race, things didn't look too good for Vogal. About three laps into the 8-lap race, she began to fall behind. It was clear that the earlier races had taken their toll and that now it was just about finishing. No one would think any less of her; after all, it was a state championship that her team had her to thank for even being in. Five laps later Vogal was in last place. As she rounded the last turn she noticed another competitor just ahead of her and that this girl was the only thing standing between her and a last place finish. Maybe she could save a shred of her own dignity and at least not finish last, but then something happened. Vogal noticed that the only other competitor standing between her and the finish line was faltering in her attempt to finish. At this moment Vogal hit a small crossroads of her own. She could pass the girl, saving face and finishing in 14th place where she could at least say she didn't finish last, or she could help the girl cross the finish line. Doing so would mean her immediate disqualification from the race but she also knew what was more important at that time. Vogal swept in and wrapped the other runner's arms around her shoulders and helped the injured runner finish the race. Not only did Vogal help the runner, she put the other girl out in front of herself so that the injured runner would finish first. What a champ! Last place or not, who do you think won that day?

A little closer attention to what happened that day and how it relates to you as a man will disclose some amazing truths about your life as a father. As men and as fathers we are naturally looked to as a support system of strength and guidance. Our role is to be a pillar of strength, a guiding light and an anchor that allows for stability in the storms of life. If our children cannot rely on us for these traits, they are left to weather life by themselves. They are left to do this life alone when they had no control over getting here in the first place. It really is unfair. There are so many boys out there who have had to stumble along trying to figure out what manhood is because the man who helped bring them into the world refused to be the set of shoulders that boy needed to lean on to get him to the next leg of life. This failing as a father perpetuates ill-equipped competitors in the race of life and, at the very least, ensures poor runners. Likewise, there are so many young ladies out there also searching for the aforementioned qualities that should have been found in Dad, but they are searching for them in lackluster men. Those men are probably suffering from the same symptoms that so many are when their manhood examples are absent. So our precious daughters are left without a defense from the wolves whose appetite for their beauty and body is insatiable and who are constantly on the prowl for those women whose minds are weak enough to be taken advantage of. So what will you do about that? Is it in you to allow the runners on your team to falter to the point of failure? Or will you, no matter where you are in your race with them, be shoulders for them to lean on? Rest assured that the day will come when it is time to pass the baton from you to the next generation and, from that moment on, whatever foundation you have laid will be the floor that is built on to run the next leg of the race. Make your foundation sure. Make your foundation strong so you can reach forward to the next generation of leaders looking for help and offer a firm footing for them to build on.

Your biological children are not the only place you are leaving legacy. Your interactions and influence are felt everywhere you are. When light enters a dark room, no matter how large the room or how dark the room, that light can be seen at a great distance away. The funny thing about darkness is that it can't get any darker. Once all light has been removed, the darkest of darks is still only so dark. But one of the unique qualities of light is that it can always be brighter and, in the same way, as men and as fathers, we should be bringing light to every situation, everywhere we go. Change your environment. Influence it for positive change. Whether it's on the ball field or the board room, leave a legacy of Godly strength and honor that women respect and men admire.

GETTING IT COACHED UP

Every great leader is aware of his or her need to actively be doing two things at any given time. The first one is the recognition that they need help and the second is getting it. There is strength in numbers, or "...in a multitude of counselors, plans succeed." (Prov. 15:22). Every great leader on the planet has a dedicated team of advisors and it is a practice that dates back for centuries. Kings, pharaohs, presidents, prime ministers, you name it. If there was a high leader, there was a high counsel. The president of the United States has several counselors around him advising him on any number of issues at any given time and I would argue that a man's position in his home is even more important than the president's in government. In fact, the failure of men in the home affects the country in a way that makes it necessary for a president to have to step-in, in certain circumstances. So if the president needs counselors and our job is more important than his, how much more do you think we need counselors as men and as fathers? How much more do we need accountability and a band of brothers to rely on to do life with successfully?

The point here is that you can't do this thing alone. Understanding and accepting this truth is critical to your success as a father. You will need people to be close confidants with as well as people who can give you valuable wisdom and advice in areas that inherently you may not have as a strength. These people will give you the proper tools to make informed decisions in life; offering advice on things like leading your home and raising your children but also in general areas like how to advance in business, where to get your car fixed and so on. They will also pick you up when you are down and hit you with tough love when you need it most. Many of these people will be close friends and should be. These are the people who are allowed to look into your life and usually know a little bit more about you than other casual friends you have. They care, and are genuinely invested in your life in some capacity. However, some of them may not necessarily be so. They might come in the form of a pastor or a business associate. It might be the guy at the gas counter; who knows? If you are keeping your ears and heart open, if you are actively pursuing wisdom, then you never know where it will come from. You'll be surprised where you will get wisdom from when you are looking for it. The key is to be looking and willing to hear it when it presents itself to you.

Reaching back, proverbially speaking, to get help, is a recognition of one's own limited ability. In being a dad it is no different. Resourcing information from a variety of sources is not an admission of a lack of understanding as much as it is a type of reconnaissance for the mission ahead. It can get really overwhelming, really fast—exponentially so when you adopt the attitude of being a loner. The lone wolf syndrome is a trap and a lie to get you isolated and alone. Sure, it looks cool on screen or on paper but rarely works out in real life. Did you know that even wolves hunt in packs? And the gazelle that leaves the herd gets picked off. It is a principle that is as true in civilization as it is in the wild. Superheroes are greater when they have other superheroes around them for support and together they are usually unstoppable, even if one temporarily goes down. Even Jesus surrounded himself with twelve others not only to teach but to be comforted by. The disciples recognized their need for him but Christ also knew how he would need them in return.

Therefore, the first you need to do is to be reaching back. In other words be reaching out for help in some capacity. You cannot help anyone else if you yourself are a mess. The second thing to do is to be actively reaching forward. You might think that the default nature of parenting is reaching forward to pass the baton to the next generation but if you are not actively and deliberately making a concerted effort to leave a legacy with your children, then having the title of "Dad" alone is not going to get it done. We have plenty of those examples in dads who were physically present but were emotionally and spiritually withdrawn. Don't be them. Reach back for the help that you need so your ground is solid enough to stand on. Then reach forward to help those who are learning to stand on their own and relying on your example to help them do it. The result is a lasting legacy that you will be honored because of. If a high school girl can see the worth in putting another before her, even in last place, then a grown man, a man on a hero's journey should be able to make that connection as well.

CHAPTER SEVEN
INITIATE, INSTIGATE AND AGITATE
TIME TO SMASH!

There is a famous saying that we have all probably heard that comments on the general state of nobility in men. "Chivalry is dead." Have you heard it before? A quick search on-line will turn up a few definitions of the word "chivalry", all of which I like and all of which have a great deal to do with men.

> *Chivalry: noun*
> • *the combination of qualities expected of an ideal knight, esp. courage, honor, courtesy, justice, and a readiness to help the weak.*
> • *the medieval knightly system with its religious, moral, and social code.*
> • *courteous behavior, esp. that of a man toward women.*
> • *courage, honor, courtesy, justice, and a readiness to help the weak.*

Now, when you think about the men in the world today who are being celebrated as "real men" at least in a public and media driven way, and look at the definition above, is the current representation of manhood in this day and age lining up with the definition? No? Not sure? Let's make it personal then because we can't control what anyone else does. When you look at your own life, even if it's the man and father that you are aspiring to be, is this same man lining up with the definitions above? If so then great! You have an awesome foundation to build a house on, but if not then why or why not? Over the course of the last few generations men have forgotten what is means to be a man or, worse yet, we have never learned. We have lost our nobility and our honor. We have also lost three key areas of strength that are crucial to successful leadership in the home. Men do not know how to initiate, instigate and agitate the world around them in a positive way. Sure, men have learned that they should initiate things like sex but on their own terms without the consideration of their wife's feelings. Men have learned how to instigate fights with their family members but not how to instigate positive change. Men have also learned how to agitate their children but not in a capacity that builds up and challenges for the sake of growth and legacy but in a capacity the sets the expectation unreachably high.

The level of effectiveness that men and fathers have in instigating change in the recent generations has been dying off and is now under threat of being endangered. Feminism has empowered women to a fault and weakened men to passivity. Men want a lady in the streets and a freak in the bed but have neither provided for that lady from those streets nor committed to the home that houses that bed. The modern man's idea of intimacy begins with an "S" and ends with "X" and society has caught on, so much so that even commercials are selling products purely with sex. I recently saw a hamburger commercial that was so heavily laden with sexual innuendo (because what sells burgers better than a half-naked girl eating charred mammal flesh, dripping condiments all over herself?) that I feared allowing my children to be in the room with me while it was on. Working directly in the marketing and advertising industry myself, I could not help but wonder why they would think that was a good idea, but then it hit me. They are doing it because a male audience is responding to it.

Men are voting with their feet and with their dollars and the standard of what is being tolerated on television and in real life is getting lowered and lowered all the time.

This cycle has been going on for some time. When generation after generation of true manhood has eroded and then been passed on, soon enough manhood and the tasks that lie within it become a figment of imagination. Ideologies of what true manhood is are created from imagination and passed on from individuals who have no basis of comparison to establish an accurate view of what it is supposed to look like. So, instead of a modeled example, young boys are left trying to figure it out from other young boys who also don't have a clue. When emotional and physical impulse takes precedence over sacrifice and servanthood, true manhood becomes a thing of the past; honorable fathering is no more because of the level of inconvenience these traits present to our self-centered life. After all, "It's simply not natural to be with just one woman," I have heard. This type of logic degrades the fabric of manhood and fatherhood and reduces it down to primal impulse. The line between man and animal fades to grey allowing for all manner of definition and prominent ideas of the day to prevail. But what does it matter? We are all just advanced monkeys anyway, right? Or advanced versions of unicellular creatures? We are just returning to our roots!

But there is a problem. With all these relative views of what manhood is, there seems to be no way to accurately define and replicate it. We just know what it is not. Often I'll hear a woman say something like, "He's not a real man," as if to say, "I know what a real man looks like and he's not it." They seem to know exactly what a real man is. But if that is true because they have seen real men at work, then why is there such a great void where it should be filled with all the real men? I don't think our generation knows at all what real men look like. Remember, moving targets are hard to hit so society comes up with a "definition of the day" but when the day changes, so does the definition. If the definition is constantly changing then we are continuously having to start over. If we are constantly starting over then what are we left with? We are left with impulse and whim guiding generations because no one can seem to give actual direction. This is leaving us with devastating results.

TIME TO SHAKE THINGS UP

So what is the answer? How do we solve these issues and change the trajectory of our sons? As some men have understood for centuries when faced with adversity that threatens their family and their own well-being, there are only two solutions. You either allow the tides of day to shift and take you where they may or you get a little angry and the Hulk inside of you comes out. The one that turns green and smashes stuff when he's upset. OK, don't go breaking things around your house. You get what I am saying. This is the guy who has to buckle his chinstrap, bull his neck and dip his shoulder so that he can push his way through the opposite direction of culture. I am talking about a fight. Not passively engaging in a fight because there was no other choice, but aggressively turning your face towards the opposition and laying a right hook directly in its mouth! A man must take the position that says not only will he not go with the crowds; he won't stand to be pushed in that direction either.

You have to be determined not to go in the direction of the masses when it comes to being an epic man or a father. In fact, I would dare to say that, in order to be a great father, you must rarely be a part of the masses when it comes to shaping your thoughts and actions around the ideas of manhood and fatherhood or any important philosophy in your life. It doesn't mean you cannot learn from what's being offered, but what it does mean is examine the evidence and the outcomes of the proposed ideas that surround fatherhood, consider the source and its motivations and make deliberate and informed decisions. Proceed cautiously when society is headed in a direction of thought or action and you are following that same direction. Going in the direction that the majority goes in isn't necessarily wrong but stands to be more in the "relative" category as in "what's good for you may or may not be good for me" than the correct view of biblical male headship. The term "correct" can even come into question in the "light" relativity, so you can see how it becomes a slippery slope very quickly. Unfortunately, in this day and age, this seems to be the mantra of society. A resounding voice of relativism. Truth cannot be relative, however. Truth can only be one of two things; that is, indeed true or nothing at all. Truth cannot be governed by what society deems appropriate at the time otherwise there is no standard by which we can govern our own behavior, ever. Relative truth cannot be judged properly because if it is relative then one person's view on any one thing can never be wrong at any point in history. Most people would see the abuse of children as wrong but the society that is governed by relativism cannot take a moral stand on such an issue because what is wrong to them may not be wrong to the person doing this horrible act. The very statement "that there is no truth" is fundamentally flawed because the statement itself is a truth claim. So if "there is no absolute truth" in regard to any subject or belief system, then the statement itself is also untrue, making it false. Allowing a society who is ruled by relativism to govern our ideas of manhood, marriage and parenting leaves gaping holes in the original plan of fatherhood that God set out for us when He created us as men.

So how can a man make any solid decisions to lead and know that, without a shadow of doubt, he is making the right decision? He must lead the way in living out his example of time-tested, God-honoring principles. He must be an example that does not conform to the status quo and he must challenge his family to do the same. He must pursue this with reckless abandon unless he is pulled in the direction of passivity. Passivity is dangerous because it has a tendency to turn to apathy, which then leads to the death of manliness.

> "What good is salt if it's lost it saltiness? It is no longer good for anything except to be thrown out..."

Matthew writes this in chapter 5:13 of his book. In the same way, if a man loses his manliness to passivity he has become good for nothing. Leading and offering strength is in the very nature of who we have been created to be as men and as fathers. If we are not pursuing and nurturing it feverishly then we are allowing it to atrophy and we have made ourselves susceptible to attack—and the attack on God-given masculinity is great, not only from within ourselves but from the very real enemy of our souls. If the devil can get us to be passive in our function as men, if he can get us to stop leading, or to lead in a direction that is contrary to God's purpose, then he immobilizes our potential for greatness in our sphere of influence. The impact that this has obviously relays to our families but also alters the unseen and innumerable amount of ripple effects that our life can potentially be generating.

BEING PETER PARKER IS NOT BEING PETER PAN

There is a condition currently plaguing young adults born in the late '80s and early '90s that is so prevalent in current culture that a name has been given to it. The medical industry has referred to it as a recognizable condition though it is not as of yet being considered a psychopathology. It is called "Peter Pan Syndrome". The condition is currently being defined as a situation wherein the person is exhibiting behavior and emotions that do not allow them to mature as adults. It is literally prohibiting their ability to handle adult responsibilities. There is an adult body with childish behaviors. It's a bit convenient if you ask me but I am not a doctor. It is mainly affecting young people in western cultures and, though both sexes are affected, the majority of those affected are men. No big surprise there. There are literally millions of young men in the world today who are refusing to grow up for one reason or another. There was a time when growing up was not a choice, or a medical condition for that matter. There has never in history been this kind of mass outbreak against the responsibilities of manhood. As a society, we love the title but not the job. Most cultures throughout history have embraced it and celebrated the crossing over into it, but we are at a place where true manliness is so feared and shunned by young and old men alike that the medical world is taking notice. Some interesting characteristics of the condition, besides the inability to take on responsibility, are the inability to keep promises, excessive care about the way they look (on the outside), a lack of self-confidence, though they don't seem to show it and actually come across as exactly the opposite. Sound like anyone you know? This same syndrome is carrying over into how men view and approach dating and marital relationships.

Studies are showing that fewer and fewer people desire marriage though they still desire children. What this comes down to is a lack of desire to officially commit to one person for the rest of their lives and to do it in a capacity that solidifies the commitment and is recognized before God and man. We want our legacy to live on in our children but we don't want to have to actually show them what that looks like in a committed relationship. Since many people subscribe to the idea that God doesn't exist or that there are many paths to God, it is easy to see how eliminating His statutes of marriage, or selectively choosing the ones they like and disregarding the ones they do not, could easily happen.

Since mankind is generally self-seeking in his inclinations, there is a disregard for the origins and purpose of time-honored traditions like marriage. Instead, modern generations prefer objective morality in the name of "progress". In spite of the effect of this philosophy, we believe our way is better. Our trial run of marriage with no real commitment waiting at the end is the contemporary solution to better relationships and better parenting even though the stats are saying just the opposite.

We are living with a generation that is obsessed with self. Self-centered religions, self-centered ambitions, and #selfies. People can loosely see the point in having children, though even that is on the decline, but they don't see the point in marriage anymore. The irony here is that studies show that generally people still believe that raising a child with two loving parents is better than one. But how does this even make sense if the modeled example of love shown by two parents shows no real commitment to each other? Today's type of commitment says, "I'll love you enough to be with you forever, *conditionally*; but not enough to marry you, *forever.*" Why should people align themselves with an antiquated tradition that also seems to marginalize those who don't fit in the status quo? If people are doing everything that married people do without committing then what is the point? We can have sex. We can live and pay bills together. We can even parent children so why not accept being married? It's just piece of paper and we are already doing everything that married folks do, right?

I believe the reason is that men and women have become afraid of commitment and of being vulnerable. We fear the responsibility and work that marriage requires. There is also a sense of finality we don't like. We don't like the idea of "forever" with anything, let alone being married to someone forever. To some, the idea of "forever" is a romantic and consoling notion yet to others, it strikes fear in their hearts. Many of these people have had horrible examples of marriage shown to them during their upbringing so their fear is that what they saw modeled will be what happens to them. So why do young adults not commit to marital relationships? Because, psychologically, there is a door out, an escape that says, "If this doesn't work out, then at least we won't have to get a divorce." An even worse philosophy to have is, "If this marriage doesn't work out then we'll just get a divorce." It is no wonder this generation wants to stay as young as it can for as long as it can.

But modern generations have it backwards. They say, "We'll do a trial run on this marriage without being married, to see if we want to get married," and as a result this process has undermined intimacy, further destroying any sentiment of chivalry that may have been formed by establishing a relationship built on commitment. This mindset has had a horrendous effect on relationships in the last 50 years and it stands to affect the next 150 years if something doesn't change.

The attitude that says it opposes marriage is not the only factor involved. To say that the Internet, social media and technology have not had a significant and adverse influence on relationships and marriage would be misguided. The dwindling desire to marry coupled with amount of access we now have as a result of technology has given people a false sense of invincibility when it comes to relationships. This is because people now have more ways to meet other people than ever before so if one relationship doesn't work, they can easily find another. It has led us to believe that we always have a way around true commitment. There has been a progressive and steady falloff in the "desire to be married" category in recent history and the emotion of fear is a strong stakeholder in its demise. However, the common theme that is even more central than fear, is that **the fear lies in the heart of men**.

MEN LEAD THE WAY WHETHER THEY WANT TO OR NOT

Where the majority of men go, a society will follow, no matter how misguided they may be. When in the 1950s, '60s and '70s the marriage-minded philosophy of men collectively changed from honoring their wives and children to the pursuit of sexual freedom, women soon thereafter adopted the same idea—I think partly out of retaliation for having been mistreated in the position of homemaker but also partly because of the desire to be freed from their own responsibilities as homemakers as well. The irony is that there are many women who will tell you that, in their heart of hearts, though now they are fully integrated in every aspect of corperate America, they have never really let go of the desire to take care of their home or to be married. The idea of being married, in woman's heart, speaks to a sense of worth and value over her life and has done so for centuries. But, again if men don't want it, society will follow.

Men, by design, are anointed with the responsibility of leadership even if they do not own it. So if a man does not want to get married, that idea has the potency to change a society. The same is true for other areas of his life as well. Studies have shown that if the father in a home does not want go to church or study the Bible, his children are more likely not to want to go to church and will be likely to grow up without any view on who God is. If a man does not want to father his children then they will likely not even want children of their own out of fear of being like their lackluster father. Whatever way a man leads his family in, it is likely that they will follow in some capacity. Stats prove all of these above statements to be true and this is a scary thought.

Remember, these are the prevailing thoughts only in western cultures. While we as Christian men are delaying our responsibilities as husbands and fathers, young Muslims in Europe, Asia and the Middle East are embracing them and raising large families that will carry their ideas and philosophies to impact the generations to come and they will have exponential numbers to support these ideas with. Homosexual couples desire marriage now more than ever and are being granted it, while heterosexual couples desire individualism more than ever. Governments around the world are making allotments and accommodations for all of these demographics in effort to appease the masses and it's all coming to a boiling point. All these repercussions are the results of a lack of Christ-centric leadership, impotent male headship and male passivity. These are the outcomes of generation after generation of men opening the door to relativism and allowing the enemy to have his influence by way of passive or overbearing leadership. Neither style is centered around love, commitment or sacrifice and both have devastating effects.

So what does "male headship" look like then? Is it the shady political leader who has affairs on the side while smiling and lying through his teeth about his position on a certain policy? Is it the greasy tele-evangelist who stands to benefit from your $1000 donation though he says blessings and favor will flow your way if you'll just "sow a seed"? Did I mention this guy also has affairs on the side that are homosexual and/or prostitution related? He's a real upstanding citizen and the picture of strong male,

Christ-centric leadership (insert sarcastic tone here). Or maybe it looks like a drunk who beats on his wife and is living up to his T-shirt's title. Maybe that same dad, whom you have envisioned to be a superhero at some point, is more like a super bum on the couch. He can't hold a job, his wife doesn't respect him and his children can't stand him. Or maybe it's completely the opposite. Maybe it's the super-rich entertainer who has no need to commit because he has all the money in the world and every beautiful model at his beck and call. He drops one girl and is on to the next in a matter of phone calls. Is this what male headship is supposed to look like? Is this the picture of masculinity we have? If, in your eyes, this is what you think male headship is, it is no wonder why you would not want anything to do with those kinds of leaders. "No thanks!" right? Maybe you're saying something like this, "I have determined that I am never going to be like those guys so I'd rather not do anything at all just in case it ends up looking like them." All those guys are pretty awful people with the exception of the wealthy playboy, right? But, then again, if you have everything that life can offer you, like wealth and fame, but you lose your soul, what's it all worth? So he's not that great either. Well, who could blame you for feeling the way you do?

BEING THE HEAD AND NOT THE TAIL

These examples are not you! They are not who you are going to be. You are a part of a new generation of men, the proud and the few who will go against the flow of the masses and will face the odds that are increasingly not in your favor. You are the kind of man who, in the eyes of women and children, is raised to the status of "superhero" though you don the apparel of an ordinary man. In an interview on male leadership, Pastor Voddie Baucham put it like this:

> *"Male headship is not about lording it over those whom we lead. Male headship is about being so Christ like that it is evident to everyone around us that we are the head*

> *of our home. Male headship is about being the spiritual priest, the spiritual prophet, the physical provider and the physical and spiritual protector of our households. That is what male headship is. Male headship is laying down your life for your wife. That is what male headship is. If she is afraid of you, you are not operating under biblical male headship. And if you are not mentoring and discipling your wife, you are not operating under biblical male headship. It is your responsibility according to Ephesians chapter five to wash her with the water of the Word. Are you washing your wife in the word, sir? Then don't you dare pound your chest and say that you are the head of anything. Are you bathing your wife in prayer, sir? Then don't you dare say that you are her head from a biblical perspective. Male headship is not about dominating women. It is about realizing that they are weaker vessels with whom we have been entrusted and for whom we are called to lay down our lives literally if necessary. That is male headship. And I will not apologize for that. That is what we are called to operate in men."*

So what does it mean to initiate, instigate and agitate? It means to go first. It means to lead out by example even if fear exists in your heart. It means to shake up the status quo and do things differently than popular culture even if everyone else around you abandon's your philosophy. Leading in this capacity inspires those who are looking for true strength in leadership. You will never lead those who are not willing to follow but you will never have followers if you are not willing to lead. You must step out and determine to be different than what you have seen and experienced. Your experience is not a sentencing of your future. Ephesians chapter five verse twenty-five is a good place to start. Lead with love. Lead with the Word. Lead with righteousness and selflessness. Lead by serving. When you physically do these things there will be changes in your atmosphere. Your children will respond with you differently. Your wife will respond with you differently. You will feel different. You will feel pretty dang amazing when it all starts to come together.

It is hard. There is no question about it. Pain is a part of being a man as growing pains are a part of growing up. But it is worth it. It might be easy to say, "Well, I don't know how, I didn't have a dad or an example to show me how." Then you need to find an example that you look up to and get to work or be daring enough to shape your own example and unafraid to make mistakes along the way. Stop looking for excuses as to why you can't do it and look for ways you can. You need to resource yourself with a person/coach or books or information so that you can be well-equipped for the task ahead. Don't think for one second that it will be an overnight transformation either. Educating yourself to be the man you are trying to be will be a lifelong pursuit that will have incremental advances but over time you will grow and when you look back after some time you will see how far you have come.

There is nothing magical, mystical, or spiritual that is going to automatically make you a man of God when you get married. Marriage will not make you a man but this doesn't mean you should back down from the challenge. It is going to take some downright hard work to be the man, husband and father you want to be. It will be work to lead your wife spiritually. It will be work to love and train your children with discipline. However, fearing failure is not an option when it comes to leading. Remember that, by doing nothing, you are doing something so if you fail to lead then you are leading in failure. Face your fears eye to eye and don't go down without a fight. In addition, don't be afraid of not being spiritually "ahead" of those who have been entrusted to you to lead. You might be saying, "My wife is spiritually stronger than me so how can I lead her spiritually?" If that is the case then the battle is half won with you recognizing that she is ahead of the game. Thank God she is on your team and then get to work on your spiritual life because the balance of your wife being ahead of you is only going to work for so long. Eve was made from Adam's rib. Ribs are a last ditch effort to protect your vital organs from taking on serious damage but they break easily if under constant or sharp pressure. Your wife is an incredible safety mechanism for your heart but you must protect her lest you put yourself in harm's way. Allowing your wife to be ahead of you spiritually can only last for so long. You won't enjoy it and neither will she. If you are being the man you need to be by initiating, instigating and agitating and she is seeking the Lord as well then she will naturally respond to your leadership since you will be modeling it for her, serving her and loving her in it. As men, it is better for us to fail in an attempt to lead our wives spiritually than not be spiritually leading at all.

The world is quick to point out the problems it has with Christian doctrine and it is also quick to try to separate people from their dollars. But secular thinking can be pretty self-aware as well. So maybe it is not too ironic when an advertising company, whose sole function is to find creative ways to separate us from our dollars while staying as politically correct as they can, designed an ad with a politically incorrect world view that is all too spot on. I came across this Dockers commercial and I thought it summed up this chapter pretty well so I'll end this one "with a word from the sponsors!"

> *Once upon a time, men wore the pants and wore them well. Women rarely had to open doors, and little old ladies never had to cross the street alone. Men took charge because that is what they did, but somewhere along the way the world decided it no longer needed men.*
>
> *Disco by disco, latte by foamy non-fat latte, men were stripped of their khakis and left stranded on the road between boyhood and androgyny; but today, there are questions our genderless society has no answers for.*
>
> *The world sets idly by as cities crumble, children misbehave, and those little old ladies remain on one side of the street. For the first time since bad guys, we need heroes. We need grown-ups. We need men to put down the plastic forks, step away from the salad bar, and untie the world from the tracks of complacency. It is time for you to get your hands dirty. It is time to answer the call of manhood.*

It is time to wear the pants.

~Harris, Alex and Bret. www.therebelution.com.
December 2009. Web. May 15th, 2014

Do not straddle the fence of adolescence and manhood, gentlemen, but step up full force into it and embrace the responsibilities you get to have as a man. It is an honor to have been given these tasks. Celebrate them and rejoice in them. You have been created to handle them and no one can lead exactly like you can, so get to it! Let the mean green guy out, and don't be afraid to get messy. They may not like you when you're angry but they'll love you when you are in control.

CHAPTER EIGHT
SHOW UP AND SHOW OUT
HEROES SHOW UP TO SAVE THE DAY.

When I was in high school we used to have a saying that me and my friends would use whenever somebody was doing whole a lot of "extra" wherever it was not necessarily needed. We would say something like this: "Man, Ralph was really *showing out* on the field today!" Or "Bro, Travis is always trying to *show out*!" It wasn't a reference that was made with a negative connotation. It was just an expression to show that we recognized the "above and beyond" attitude that our circle of misfits was so fond of displaying.

Later in life, as a photographer, I had many opportunities to document special events in people's lives. One of the events that I was quite fond of doing was graduation ceremonies. They are special events for many reasons but one of the main reasons I liked shooting them so much was just the sense of accomplishment and achievement that you could literally see on the graduates' faces as they walked across the stage. Each student would cross the stage with their individual style, some with a graceful glide, and others with a skip and a shout, but any way it went down, it was fun to watch each person enjoy these few moments that they had worked so long for. This experience could only be topped by any friends or family in the audience who would be screaming and shouting at the top of their lungs. You know these crazy people. They are the ones with noisemakers and signs, fog horns or just voices that seem to project so loudly that they fill the room like fog horn. Some folks would be so loud that you would cringe in embarrassment for a split second even though afterwards you kind of wished someone was making that big a fuss about you. These people would definitely be categorized as *showing out*! Their voices were so infectious, so radiant with pride and excitement that it would literally change the mood of the room from somber observers to joy filled participants. They were proud and rightly so. They were cheerleaders for the person they were there for. They were a spectacle of support and wanted everyone to know that the person crossing the stage was worth making a scene over and that their pride in that person was so great that sometimes all you can do is *show out*! As men and as fathers, we should be the same way.

THEY SEE YOU BUT CAN THE FEEL YOU?

The pandemic of absent fathers doesn't only apply to the homes that do not physically have a man there. There are plenty of homes with a large heap of an ogre, who occupies the space but mentally and surely spiritually has checked out. In this regard, the presence of a real man is absent in that home as well. This is extremely confusing and sometimes even worse than not having a man physically present at all. The reason is because the message is conflicting. They can see you but they don't feel your effects. It is even worse if the only effects you deal out are negative or punishment related. Remember what I was saying earlier about "manning up"? The expectation is one that says, there are jobs that only "a man" can do or that only "a man" should do but when the one guy who is supposed to fill that role is around but is not doing those things, well, what good is he? It would be better if he were not even around. At least that way the excuse would be valid. If you are present and not doing the things that you should be doing in your home or in your family's life, rest assured that they are feeling the effects of your lack of "showing out".

In every aspect of family life there is a large gap that should only be filled by Dad. It can, however, be filled by all sorts of other things. Distractions like technology, television, drugs, premature teen or premarital sex, misbehavior, chaos and all manner of other issues are examples of things that are waiting just outside of Dad's jurisdiction. If Dad is not showing up to set the tone for these areas then these other things are. It's just the way it is and it has been playing itself out in our society for decades. Stats prove it, society and real life prove it and the Bible has been proving it over and over for centuries. Even with Dad in place, challenges still arise so how much more do the problems arise if the man who is supposed to be playing this role decides to check out?

Men are supposed to be immovable foundations that a house can be built on. Men are supposed to be reliable and durable. We'll talk more about this later but for now I will say that if you are not married with kids yet then you are in the process of solidifying the type of man you will be. If you are married then your foundation of manhood is being looked to and relied on for support. Finally, if you have kids, your foundation of manhood is actually being built on as we speak. For some guys out there this might be a bit disconcerting because you are still in the process of establishing the strength of your foundation. The good news is that foundations can have flaws and at times may need repairs. It's the ones that are cracked all the way through due to low or no maintenance that are no good. It's the foundation that moves that cannot be trusted to support the weight of a building or a home.

JESUS AT THE CENTER OF IT ALL

Men must show up and then show out to be an active presence in our families' lives. It's not enough to just be physically present in the home. We must be spiritually and mentally present and stirring things up. We must make a clear and concerted effort to be an active and dynamic part of each of our family members' lives starting with our own relationship with God, then our relationship with our wife and finally our relationship with our children and it must be in that order.

A relationship with Jesus Christ is central to everything I am speaking about in this book. If you don't know anything about this man, who he is or why he is important, then skip forward to the last chapter. If you do know this man and are on a journey to be more like him then you know that his love for you is great. So great, in fact, that there aren't any books in existence that can expound on it in its entirety. Many have tried and done a great job, however most of those books are just commentary on what the Bible has been talking about forever. The Bible is, perhaps, the best at revealing to us the complexity of God's love for us. In the Bible there is lesson after lesson of God, the ultimate father, giving us practical advice on how to be strong in the midst of trial and how drawing close to Him is key to being the man that He has called each and every son of His to be.

One year, I was in a limousine, on my way to a good friend's wedding. In the car was my friend, my friend's dad (whom I greatly admired for being a man's man and a Godly man at that) and myself. We used to call him "Pops" as he was most often the only "man/dad"-like figure my small gang of miscreants had to look up to. Pops turned to my friend, his son, and asked him, "Are you ready?" and, nervously, as any groom is on his wedding day, my friend replied, "Yeah, I guess. I just really want to honor my wife in this relationship and be the man I am supposed to be," to which Pops replied, "Honoring your wife is easy if you'll honor God first." I'll never forgot those words. At the time I wasn't even married yet but I knew that the advice was sound and would later ring true in my own life.

For the first couple of years of my marriage, like many marriages, we were in what I like to call a "gelling" phase. I like to call it that because I played sports for most of my school years. Many athletic teams often refer to an early period of time when the players are becoming acclimated to each other's playing style, a "gelling phase". Much like sports, marriage can feel like an athletic and competitive event. Since my wife and I are on the same team we had to go through the woes of acclimating to each others style of living. It wasn't fun or easy but it was necessary. In many of the rough times, however, Pops' piece of advice would come up in my mind. I knew that if I could somehow honor God in the situation, He would allow us to resolve our differences and become more unified.

I had heard the analogy of marriage being like a triangle where the bottom two points are you and your spouse. The apex, which is also the third point, is God and the closer the two other points draw to him, the closer the two points get to each other. How true this has been in our lives. Through the rough spots we were both seeking God and relinquishing our issues with each other to Him. By letting go of these things and allowing full submission to God to take place in our lives, over the course of the second year of our marriage, something broke. I literally watched God do incredible work in the life our marriage, so much so that the woman I had in my house was literally a new woman. I did not know who she was but I did not care because the work of restoration was so sweet that I didn't want to go back to the way it used to be. What I did know was that God was involved in this change because trying to make changes on my own prior to relinquishing our relationship totally to Him was unsuccessful. Submitting myself to Christ and allowing Him to change me was critical. When I took the focus off of praying for God to change her, and allowed God to change me, that is when change with us occurred. This moment in our lives together has been vital to the success of our marriage ever since.

In 1 Peter 3:7 the Bible says this:

> "Likewise, husbands, live with your wives in an understanding way, showing honor to the woman as the weaker vessel, since they are joint heirs with you of the grace of life, so that your prayers may not be hindered."

Don't get tripped up on the "weaker vessel" part. I already addressed that earlier but even if I had not addressed it, there is a general understanding that women are not viewed as being physically stronger than men. I believe this is the reference the writer is making here. However there are two other things that are worth noting in this verse. Firstly, that woman are "joint heirs", which first means that they will share in the reward that God has for all of those who believe in Him; that they are not less than, but equal to us as men in their eternal value to God. Secondly, that God actually says that he can't even hear your voice if your relationship with your wife is off. So that brings me to my next point.

I mentioned this before but it's worth saying again. If your relationship with your wife is out of order, if there is strife between the two of you, then there can be no God-structured order in your home. If you don't have the support of the one person in the world who is supposed to have your back then your confidence will be sabotaged even before you have an attempt at establishing it. Solidifying your relationship takes work. Not only does it take work it may take counseling. I think some men think of counseling as a sign of defeat or admitting weakness because they are getting help. I think that line of reasoning is the most foolish and uninformed way of looking at it. Getting counseling should be referred to as "getting coached". There is no great athlete or team that arrived at that title without the assistance of someone else helping them get there. Michael Jordan had Phil Jackson, the Green Bay Packers had Vince Lombardi and you have every marriage resource you could ever need or imagine at the touch of a couple of buttons in your phone. Within a few minutes you could have Amazon send you a bunch of books on how to get closer to your spouse. Shortly after that you could Google "date ideas" as well as find babysitters in a couple of clicks. In nanoseconds you can tap into any well-known church's media archive and check out any videos or podcast messages on bettering your relationship and, while you are at it, you can sign up for that weekend conference that she's been wanting to go to. Total amount of time taken? Five minutes.

Do you think it's worth the investment? The point is that there are so many resources available to us in this day and age that there is no excuse for not deepening your relationship with your wife. The benefits of establishing unity in this relationship trickle down to your children and your relationship with them as well. If they can see Mom and Dad as a happy unit then their chances of spiritual and emotional success are substantially greater than if you don't practice what you preach.

Establishing these relationships could easily be categorized as a tortuous and laborious task if you wish to see it that way. However, I like to look at them as opportunities for Dad to be the father he needs to be and the superhero that everyone else in his family wants him to be. Each instance of showing up and showing out is an opportunity for you to drive a wedge in between you and the stats that are calling your family's name.

So don't just show up to the game, show up in school colors with a sign and noise makers. Don't be the shirtless painted guy in the below zero temps though, that's just ridiculous. But you know what? If that's what it takes, by all means. Don't just take her to a dinner and a movie like you've done hundreds of other times. Tell her a week in advance that you have planned something special, don't tell her what it is though. Then, if you haven't already planned something, actually go and plan something special to do and do this often. Make it fun in your own creative ways. Celebrate your family in every aspect of life. Mourn or show genuine emotion of some kind when there needs to be so that they can see your humanity and empathy for their situation. Listen more than you speak. When you do speak, let your words be few and seasoned with love, delivered with caution. Likewise, when the moment calls for it, and even when it doesn't, rejoice and cheer over the little things, no matter how many "participation" ribbons the kids bring home. Take a spontaneous road trip or an impromptu dinner one night. Buy cookies one night, or bake 'em from scratch even. It doesn't always mean you have to spend money. Show them you care in every season of life and do it on a regular basis. Each instance is a chance for you to make a deposit in the superhero category. It doesn't hurt in the "I want to make more love to my wife" category either. That's a first-hand testimony by-the-way.

WARNING: You cannot do this stuff for just one week and think they'll get it or that you have arrived, but make it a part of your title. "This is Dad, and it's just what he does." "This is my husband, and it is just who he is." Don't we all want to hear that about us? Each day is a gift to you so make it a gift to them as well. Don't wait till a holiday or special occasion to buy gifts. Those gifts are expected and almost obligatory but watch their faces of admiration light up as you go above and beyond and buy them a "just-because" gift. You'll be a fuller man because of it and you'll also be raised so high in the eyes of your family that any one of the Avengers would seem like the tooth fairy when compared to your glory.

And, finally, when it is time to graduate some of your young people off into the real world, be in the crowd, louder than anyone else, with fog horns and signs showing the world how proud of them you are and that you don't mind making a spectacle of it. What you won't see is how proud they are of you and that they get to call you Dad.

CHAPTER NINE
MAKE THE TOUGH CALLS
WITH GREAT POWER COMES GREAT RESPONSIBILITY.

I never used to want to be a leader. I never used to want to be responsible for other people or looked at as a role model. The reason was because I was too familiar with myself and my own faults to feel worthy enough to be an example for others to look at. What I didn't realize until much later was that being a man and being a leader are synonymous whether I liked it or not. Throughout the course of time, for the most part, men have been looked to first for the solutions of the world's greatest problems both big and small. Sure, there are plenty of men who get overlooked for any number of reasons but it's usually because they have become passive or non-existent in their position. A male is not man until he shows up to make the tough call. The attributes of responsibility and manhood go hand-in-hand and the duty is not voluntary. Some men choose to lead well and others avoid any semblance of the task but, either way, when you are dubbed a male at your mother's ultrasound, you are destined for some kind of leadership. As I have already said, doing nothing in regard to your leadership is, in fact, doing something.

So why is it that so many men are backing down from their God-given responsibilities? Why have so many chosen to take the easy route instead of the road less traveled? First, I think the enemy knows that when a man determines within himself to be a God-fearing man of strength and valor, people's lives can be dramatically altered for the better, so he does whatever he can to alter that man's decision making process. Also, when a man decides to be the best man he can be, it affects everything in his reach. In addition, I also believe it is because we simply don't like making the tough calls.

THE FEAR FACTOR

The male generation that is walking the earth right now has seen time after time how openly and publicly the male species is ridiculed for their failure as men and fathers. The result is that many men have taken the back seat to their own potential. When you are on a team and the score is tied with no time left on the clock do you want the ball or do you just want to be on the winning team? It is a tough call to position yourself in a place of great sacrifice but we, as men, are equipped to do exactly that. We have been forged with strength in the very foundation of who we are in order to take these, sometimes very emotional, stands. Sure, there are going to be times where no one likes you because you missed the shot but scoring the winning point is not as important as having someone to actually take the chance at making the shot.

Fear is the driving force in most things we do not try. It is a huge tool in the arsenal that the enemy uses in crippling God's people, especially men. It is actually quite ironic when you think about it. The creation that is supposed to be the epitome of strength and dominion over all things on the earth is the very being that is so easily crippled by thoughts of things that have not yet even happened. We mask our fears in a number of ways, be it withdrawing or over compensating, but nevertheless it is fear at the root of most of our issues.

So how do we overcome the legitimate fears we have as men? How do we step out in spite of the little voice inside that says, "You can't do that; you're not good enough; you don't have enough to take care of a family's needs; you're a hypocrite"? You do what all great men do when fear arises. You don't back down and find a way to alleviate your fear; you go head on and make the best educated decisions you can in spite of the fear that may exist in your heart. Notice I said make "the best educated decisions." Being a real man is not only a show of brute force or approaching things haphazardly while leaving casualties in your bull-headed wake. It is, however, having an understanding of your strengths and weaknesses and playing towards your strengths in order for you to get the "win" you are looking for. I have a friend who isn't very handy in the home improvement sense of the word. I was teasing him about this one time and he said to me, "Hey, I don't need to know how to fix that. I just need to have the number of someone who *does* know how to fix it." There is a man who knows how to play to his strengths. Not all of us are gifted in every area, but we must be resourceful. We must work both hard and smart.

Sometimes making tough calls doesn't play well into the mind of others who do not have the same vision that you have for the responsibilities that you've been given, but those other people will not have to answer for the decisions that you make. Surrounding yourself with a variety of good council and educating yourself on any given topic before you make a decision is also what the Bible calls "counting the cost". In Luke 14:28 the writer makes a proposition in regard to this very concept. He says:

> *"For which of you, desiring to build a tower, does not first sit down and count the cost, whether he has enough to complete it?"*

The point he is trying to make here is that you should not allow yourself to get into any endeavor without first having at least a small understanding of what you are about to do. It doesn't alleviate the sense of fear that you may have while making tough decisions, though it may, however it allows you to move forward in any potential circumstance with a stronger starting point.

When David faced Goliath, it was not without fear. He was well aware of his opponent's size and stature. He was well aware of the nature of situation and the effect that it was having on his people. David could clearly see Goliath's weaponry and armor. Goliath was an enormous force to be reckoned with and these sorts of details would not have gone unnoticed. But David decided to move forward in spite of the things he could see, in spite of his brother's opposition and the lack of confidence his King Saul had in him. David did not allow the size of the problem or the surmounting odds stacked against him to impede his progress. I am sure he was intimidated but instead of backing down he went full force into battle. The Bible actually says, in Samuel 17:48, that David "...ran quickly toward the battle line to meet the Philistine." While everyone around him was backing down, running away and being crippled by the effects of fear and the unknown, David was the only one running towards the issue instead of away from it. Nobody was taking charge and leading the attack. Even Saul, the king of Israel, shows fear while consulting David. Saul lists Goliath's military resume, stating, "he has been a man-of-war since his youth." Saul was crippled and perplexed as to what exactly should be done but, surely, in his mind, David was not the answer. And yet David knew something that the rest of the Israelite army apparently did not and it is the same thing that we men must remember when faced with the job of making the tough calls. It was not a respectable and well-placed sense of fear that would keep him alive or allow the Israelites to have victory in a seemingly impossible situation, however; it was his faith in the something greater than himself that would be his sustenance. Only David's trust in God and action as a man, that supported his faith, would yield a positive result.

The story of David and Goliath plays out over only a few short verses and is often pointed out for both its real-world and metaphorical applications. In this case, David's situation profoundly parallels the lives of so many men in a position where a decision needs to be made but they are gripped by the overwhelming nature of some of these decisions. Some young men are on a literal battlefield somewhere and have other people's lives in their hands. Likewise, there are other young men who are on a spiritual battlefield with just as much at stake. These men are newly married and finding that the job of a husband is bit more than they signed up for. There are fathers who don't think they can do the job of being a dad so they are on the fence as to whether or not they will even try. These types of issues are our modern day Goliath. These are the issues that are staring men in the face while spewing out insults and listing inadequacies. These adversities mock the very nature of who we are as men and call into question our manhood.

Though many years have passed since the day this epic battle took place, the truths in this story are timeless. Some say David was around seventeen years of age when this story happened and others say he was even younger. In either case it is clear that he was young but he did not let his lack of qualifications in life be a factor in what needed to be done. His lack of experience may have not given way to better judgment but what he lacked in age and experience he gained in courage and faith. This may have contributed to his fearless demeanor. I think David, though he was flawed, was familiar with the flawless track record of the God he had in his life and this is what gave him the courage he needed to thrust himself into a seemingly perilous situation. It wasn't a blind faith that had no bearing on its source. It was actually a well-informed faith that gave him the confidence to do what needed to be done and that it was, in fact, the right thing to do.

When meeting with King Saul and hearing of all he would not be able to do, David gave his own list of accomplishments. These were the things that he had seen God get him through personally. David was not resting on the assurance of his own accolades but on the faithfulness of God's character. David knew his place and he knew who he belonged to. This knowledge allowed him to move forward confidently. When we remind ourselves of God's faithfulness we can be reassured that He is on our side.

Can you look back on your life and remind yourself of times where you knew God's hand was on you? Can you see that, regardless of the foolish situations that you have gotten yourself into, if you are still breathing even now, God is sustaining you? When we can recognize how faithful God has been in our lives, we can move forward in confidence knowing that we may make mistakes but, even in doing so, we are living out our purpose as men.

When we are afraid it is imperative to remind ourselves of the flawless nature and superior timing of God. If you are not surrendered to this God, you are extremely vulnerable and living out this very heavy life with the feeble strength of finite shoulders. Seeing God in your circumstances will seem nearly impossible. Yet, even in this place, if you were to think hard enough, I am confident that you could think of a time in your life when something bigger than yourself stepped in and intervened on your behalf. It might be a minor or a major situation but you must recognize that He is very aware of you and your circumstances and has been for some time. You may not call it "God" but you don't have to for it to be true.

God desires for you to recognize His position in your life. He desires for you to be plugged into the giver of strength for the road ahead but you must relinquish your control to Him and replace the fears you have with a well-educated faith. Then and only then will you be able to move forward. Like David's faith, your faith does not have to be blind. It can actually be incredibly well-informed, grounded in the proof of your own existence. There is no circumstance of life that is a surprise to an all-knowing God. Your tribulations as a man are small in the light of who God is and even still they can feel crushing. Remembering who your God is will be a great step in the right direction of overcoming fear and it is one that we have to practice on a daily basis.

SERVANT-LEADERSHIP

Another thing standing in the way of men making the tough call is our lack of desire to lead with a servant's heart. As men we generally like to win. We like the best that life has to offer. We like the upper not the lower. In fact, who doesn't? Given the opportunity to have a surly maid girl or a beautiful supermodel, for most men, the choice seems to be clear, right? We want the best and we want it fast. We want to be the first not the last and we want the biggest or largest amount of it that we can handle. Big house, big cars, big boats, big TVs (I'm a sucker for a large screens); you name it and, if we can get it, we would take it. I always laugh when I hear someone describe themselves or another person as "a person with expensive taste." I'm like "Who doesn't have expensive taste?" Given the opportunity to have nice things, I do not know one person on the planet who doesn't want something better—always.

But upon further examination, the best isn't always what it's cracked up to be. We see plenty of celebrities and athletes who apparently have it all, who end their own lives by suicide, drugs, or some other kind of self-induced foolishness. We see the people who are considered the cream of the crop falter just like the rest of us. So maybe having all the possessions in the world is not the key to happiness. Having the job that pays a high salary and demands all of your time may not be as amazing as it sounds in reality. Maybe being the first is actually being the last.

The Bible describes how it is our intrinsic desire to have the best of everything, however, it is often also in direct contrast to the plan that God has for our lives. It doesn't mean that we cannot or should not have nice things or expensive things but what it does mean is that our hearts must not be so centrally focused on these things that bear so little weight in the light of eternity. The pursuit of placing yourself and your own needs over those around you can jeopardize your position in the kingdom of heaven but can also stand to negatively impact your influence here on Earth.

Jesus preaches, in Matthew 19:30, that many people will be giving of themselves so much to the cause of Christ that they will actually be seen as trading loyalties to family members in exchange for their loyalty to Christ.

However what they lose by way of friendships and relationships, they gain in heavenly rewards. The point I think he is trying to make is that where great sacrifice is made there will also be great reward. Christ is the ultimate example of a servant-leader. Later on, during his crucifixion, we are reminded that no one took Jesus' life but that he "freely gave" it away. Even later Paul reminds us men that we are to do the same for our wives and ultimately our families. As men leading by example in our homes we cannot be solely preoccupied with the physical things of this world. I'm not one to subscribe to the idea that we can't have nice things as Christians, however balancing our accumulation of stuff is something that, as Christians, especially Americans, we must be mindful of. Sure, there is a certain level of relativity involved in this idea, however, your desire for earthly treasure may not need to manifest itself for it to exist. We can make idols in our hearts of things by giving them too much precedence in our lives or our minds. All the while those who are nearest and dearest to our hearts are watching and mimicking our response. Our children absorb our actions like sponges and even as adults we can find ourselves repeating the behaviors of our parents later in life. Impressions are being made constantly so what kind of impressions are you leaving in your family's life?

When I moved to Los Angeles there were several things that were a bit of a culture shock to me. I came from a pretty racially diverse upbringing so the culture shock of different people wasn't an issue but the culture of Los Angeles as a city was completely new to me. Everywhere you go, no matter what time of the day, there are just crowds of people in small spaces—small parking lots, small apartments, and small stores. It was all so new to me and, frankly, became pretty irritating before long. It's like 5 o'clock traffic inside stores as well as on the streets, only it lasts all day long everywhere you go. It gets old fast.

One evening, I needed to pick up a few groceries so I decided to make a stop at the local Trader Joe's. If you are not familiar with the brand, it is a small grocery store that has all of its own branded foods and products.

These products are geared towards a health conscious crowd that wants healthier and simpler foods at affordable prices. It's like a cousin of Whole Foods only not nearly as expensive or stuffy. Anyhow, if you have never been in one of their stores what you don't know is that the square footage of the store is nowhere near the size of a regular grocery store yet it contains most of the products that you might find in a full sized store. They are not small but they are not large either. The store sizes kind of line up with the brand's values; a lot of quality and not a lot of waste. In L.A. square footage is super expensive so it makes sense that these stores are not very big. The problem is that L.A. is extremely overcrowded and the people, at least in the part of town that I was living in, are pretty health conscious. So let's recap. A small store + a lot of people = a total shopping nightmare! Grocery shopping in Los Angles, unless you go at some really off time where no one is out, is horrible.

So I finally get to the checkout lane after doing a run at TJ's and navigating through the people traffic inside the store. The place is so crammed that even the counter space that the checkout clerk is working with is limited. I mean this guy literally has no space left on his counter and he hasn't even finished getting everything out of my cart. So the way this works is that an additional clerk or someone who is not ringing you up will start to bag all of the groceries that have been scanned even before they finish going through everything in your cart. This usually creates more space on the counter for the rest of the groceries being added to the crowded counter. As a shopper, I am usually getting ready to pay or am watching the total so I can make sure I am on budget. Out of the blue, the clerk rudely says to me, as if it were my job, "Aren't you going to help pack up your stuff?" I was caught so off guard by his statement that I quickly obliged to the scolding as if it were my job without really having a second to process what had just happened. But as I left and had a chance to think about it I started to get angry about the whole thing. I mean who does this guy think he is? Bagging my food wasn't my job, it was his and if he didn't like it then why was he working there? It bothered me for weeks after the fact, so much so that I may have avoided his lane a few times afterwards just to avoid having words with this guy the next time I saw him. I have literally thought about that situation every time I have shopped at Trader Joe's ever since it happened and I shop there on a regular basis.

The whole thing taught me a few things. First is that people in the service industry need all the help they can get. They are our modern day servants and they are bombarded with people all day long who approach them with a spirit of entitlement and it doesn't make their job any easier. Yes, this is the nature of their job but as Christians, we should make it a point to be looking for ways to serve people anyway so their occupation should have no bearing. So, in being kindred spirits with folks in the service industry, we should be extremely kind and empathetic to them because, as Christians, we have a similar call. Additionally, it is an easy way to be the hands and feet of Christ by making his love experiential and tangible. You never know. You could actually be really helping someone out in a dire situation by serving their needs. The second thing is that, though it was hard to appreciate the need that the clerk was expressing because of the way he chose to express it, he was, in fact, correct in that there was an opportunity to serve that I was missing. There was a need that I could have been helping in and I wasn't even aware of it. Sure, there are times when a father needs to be the iron fist in his home, but this fist can be covered in a velvet glove.

As men addressing other men, we can have a tendency to be a bit rough with our words. Others may see this as being too aggressive. As men entrusted with the responsibility of shaping lives, we must always be able to be gentle with those who have been entrusted to us even if in the moment there is a need for a more assertive approach. Most likely those whom we will be given charge over will be more fragile than ourselves, so great care must be taken and great love must be shown when asserting our position. The point, however, is not to exert dominance but to lead by serving, and in preferring others' needs before our own we do exactly that.

Men and fathers need to be pro-actively looking for the needs of those around them and not be afraid to get their hands dirty with the work that needs to be done in order that those needs be met. Leading by serving is an extremely effective method of ministry because it is incredibly humbling to do so. Christ's example of placing peoples need for redemption before his own desire for life is the ultimate example of sacrificial love and was probably the toughest call a man has ever had to make. Even Christ expressed his own fears of being tortured when he prayed in the garden of Gethsemane, "if it is possible, let the cup pass from me..." But, as I said earlier in this chapter, the greatest men do not avoid what needs to be done because of the presence of fear. Instead, they press onward towards the prize and they lead by example. Against all odds, against all fears and even against their self-driven desires, superheroes stand up and make the tough calls.

CHAPTER TEN
DON'T TAKE TIME, CREATE TIME
BEING RIGHT ON TIME.

I have 3 kids; 2 boys and 1 girl. My daughter is not my biological daughter and she is 8 years older than the boys. We met one evening at a creative arts rehearsal for my church. Both my wife and I were heavily involved in the creative arts ministry team at the time. My wife had previously worked professionally in the entertainment industry as a performer and a Hip Hop dancer. Naturally, she was a part of our church's dance team. I have been singing for as long as I can remember. The closest I came to doing it on any large scale was being part of group that was composed of several of my closest friends who all just so happened to be very musically talented. That group would eventually grow in popularity and accolades, so much so that it would become a Dove Award winning musical act that was well known in the Christian music industry. By the time the group got signed, however, I had decided to pursue other things that I felt God had for me. This is what led me Los Angeles and the church I was serving at. It also opened up an opportunity for me to be singing on the praise and worship team. This is where this whole story converges because this is where I met my future daughter and my future wife.

Peighton was two years old at the time. Diona, my wife, was on stage rehearsing a number for an upcoming event. At a certain time in the evening, all of the different creative arts teams would either be let go for the night or be asked to come into the main theatre for final run-through. I can't remember why I was in the main theatre but I wasn't singing. For some reason I was just there watching the dancers practice. All of a sudden I feel a tug on my pants. I looked down to find a beautiful little girl staring up at me with hands raised, as if to say, "Hey pick me up!" I looked around to see if there was anyone missing a child and it didn't seem as though there was. There was a lot of music playing and a ton of people going in and out of the theatre at the time so I figured it was probably better that I held her till someone came looking for her 'cause it looked like she was just wandering around. So I picked her up. Together we sat there, both listening to music and watching the dancers dance, clapping with the music and having a good time. After a short time, Peighton's mother, Diona, noticed that the baby was with me and, since we did not know each other at the time, quickly came over to apologize and to gather her child. This was probably one of our first interactions together. What we didn't know was that this wouldn't be our last. We would eventually be around each other constantly at gatherings, parties, events, church functions; you name it, we were together and have been ever since. This whole period of time was about a year long. After that we dated for another year.

When we decided to get married, there were many things we had to figure out but one of those things was what we were going to do about Peighton's biological father. Still in the picture but far from cooperative, he was involved enough to be a confusing influence for Peighton but not enough to be considered an ounce of a real father. Any male can create a life but only a real man can sustain it and this dude was not trying to be a real man. We tried to reach out to him to incorporate him in the upbringing process but he became more of a nuisance than anything else. It wasn't his presence in the relationship that was an issue, it was his actions. He was reckless. He would say and do things that, in the vision I had for my house, were cause for concern. This was the part that was disconcerting and that required a more strategic approach. So we sought counsel and got help from a couple of different places. One of them was a friend who happened to be a lawyer; another was the actual court system itself. One of the prerequisites in a custody battle of a blended family was a session of parental counseling with a child therapist who worked for the state and all the parents involved. Diona and I went to the session and learned a lot about blended families and how to make them work. Peighton's biological father did not show up.

My biggest take away from that session would be one that I have referenced many times since then in the upbringing of my daughter. The counselor spent a lot of time dwelling on the fact that children get caught in the middle of these battles and that they are the least at fault. It would be unfair to the child to put them in a situation that pinned them up against one parent or the other. It would also be unfair to make the child feel like they had to choose who the better parent was. This resonated with me as my upbringing wasn't that much different. My parents were divorced when I was only nine years old and I often found myself in the middle of their disputes. What the counselor offered instead was advice on establishing an environment that allowed for that child to create precious memories. The actual term he used was to create "an enriched" environment. This is a place where a child can thrive and love to be at naturally. It should be filled with love, fun, adventure, memories and good times. It doesn't mean it is void of correction, discipline or tough love, but it does mean that it is a place where the child's well-being is given a fair amount of attention. Doing this allows the child to draw their own conclusions as to where they enjoy being and, by default, the parent associated with that environment naturally becomes the favored parent. It sounds like a Jedi mind trick but it's not. If both of the separated parents are doing this at the allocated time they have with the child, then that is a win-win situation. Everyone can walk away knowing that the child is in a healthy place even though the biological parents may not necessarily be. I was determined that, in my corner at least, this would be the case. I could not control what Peighton's biological father would do, but what I could control was how my house would be ran. When it came to Peighton, I was determined to make sure she knew that, first and foremost, she was loved and valued. Secondly, within the context of a home that had a mom and a dad who loved each other, that she was a priority.

In a busy schedule of work, family and church, or any of the other normal events in life there are certain people who can naturally fall by the wayside if you are not paying attention. There are relationships that can be greatly affected and it tends to be the ones who are closest to you that will suffer. I think the nature of those relationships is that they are seen as the relationships that are always there and always will be, so it's easy for them to be taken for granted. But the truth is that they won't always be there. Parents age and pass away, children grow up and leave the house, and your wife, if you are not careful, can just as easily as you, mentally move on though she may still be physically present.

As fathers, we can get stuck in the routine of work and life and not make it a point to honor and invest in these closest of relationships. We think, "Well, hey, I am doing all this work for you guys so gimme a break!" After work or on the weekend all we may want to do is decompress, watch a game with a few friends maybe while kicking back and relaxing. Meanwhile, what really happens is the wife wants to spend time together connecting, usually by way of talking and sharing on Friday night, the kids have sporting events all day Saturday and, depending on how involved you are at church, you end up in what seems like an all-day service. BOOM! There goes your weekend. Back to the grind on Monday. Sound familiar? It is no wonder that we view spending all this time creating "an enriching" environment as so much work. It's because it is! It literally is an extension of our work week. We go from one job to the next. We go from one laborious task to another. One requires one set of brain skills while the other requires what's left.

So what are we to do? Both are legitimate concerns. On one hand you need to rest to ensure that you can continue providing for your family but, on the other, that you are investing in your family in a way that leaves legacy, raises warriors and honors God. There is no easy answer here, fellas, and, just like in the earlier chapters where Spider-man has to save both the girl and the innocent children, you have to do the same. However there is hope. You can do this, it just takes a little bit of creativity and some planning.

If you approach your family like a series of tasks to be completed it will always seem dreary and they will be put on the back burner to be left behind with the other things you have to take care of. After a while you'll lose interest and before long you'll be back to not doing anything in the first place. However, if you approach it like a challenge to overcome or a puzzle to be solved, you'll be stepping into your hero boots for the task ahead and, since you are a stud, knocking out all these birds in a single blow will be a boost to your superhero ego. The key to managing all of your responsibilities with your family is the management of the time that you have with them. Who knew that a skill set you are probably using in some capacity on a day to day basis at work would come in so handy in your family life as well? I know it's not rocket science but it doesn't have to be for men to avoid it. It just has to look like a moving target and, remember, we don't like moving targets. We like wins. So set yourself up for one.

SETTING UP YOUR WIN

Making time and not taking it is a deliberate and intentional act that is going to require some thought and planning. If you are feeling brave, then take the initiative and plan your weekends literally half hour by half hour from the time you get off of work to the time you go back. If that becomes too much of a challenge to manage on your own then go and enlist the help of your closest partner, your wife. She'll love this. She'll love that you are taking initiative, thinking about the family and admire that you are strong enough to know when you need help. Besides, she probably knows the family schedule better than you do anyway. If planning is not your thing then explain what you are trying to do to your wife and see if she wouldn't mind putting some of these plans together herself, so that your schedule is laid out for you. You'll want to be able to add or take away as needed so just keep in mind that flexibility is key. Life likes to throw curve balls all the time so not being too rigid here is critical. Remember, the whole point is to grow the relationships that matter most but that doesn't always mean you have to be out doing something. Sometimes relaxing together is just as good as doing some kind of family activity, so don't be afraid to build in that time as well. Build in time for rest. Build in time for play, quiet time and alone time for Mom and Dad. In fact, build in quiet time and alone time for your wife too. Give her an hour or two or maybe even a day where she does not have any of her normal day to day responsibilities as a mom. I dare you! Show her you value her by giving her a much needed break. It will come back in droves in one way or the other and it goes a long way in showing that you care and desire to put her needs before your own. Build in time to call the grandparents and time for whatever else you need to do that is important you as a family. Again, you'll be surprised at how much time the stuff you want to do DOES NOT take when you make it a point to be deliberate about it.

Men respond to structure and order. If you know that you have two hours of alone time to do something you enjoy, then you can plan family time around that and you'll be more apt to meet the needs of those around you because you have had some time to yourself. It's not all the time you may want but, remember, your time no longer belongs only to you so a sacrifice will need to me made. If you are having trouble with letting go of some of your free time to spend it with your family then there is an issue we need to address. When you vowed to your wife that you would love her enough to commit to her for the rest of your life, then the rights to your time became a partnership with your wife and family. In the same way we as Christians have been bought for a price. Christ has paid for your time so it no longer belongs to yourself. So this idea that your time is solely yours is something that you need to examine and pray about how you can see your situation through the lens of Christ's example.

The Bible uses the metaphor of marriage to help us understand the relationship that God has with the church. The Bible says that the church, otherwise known as the people who claim to believe that Jesus is the Son of God and follow his example, are his bride and that he is the groom. Being the man in this relationship, Christ has already laid down his life for his bride (1John 3:16), which shows us a few things. First, he has initiated this relationship by going before us and showing us, by example, how to do it. Second is that Christ's example shows the level of intensity at which he does this act of service towards us. In 1 John 15:13 the Bible says that the greatest show of love is to lay down your life for someone you care about. Any way you cut it, there is a sacrifice that needs to be made. Christ did it first and he gave everything even unto death. That is the type of act that catapults his example into epic and iconic superhero status and, since you are a hero in training here, that sacrifice is one of the first things you will need to learn how to make. Let me also mention that it should be made with every ounce of strength you have. We don't like the idea of sacrifice because the very implication is pain, discomfort and surrender. To a degree you would be correct. Yet, if you learn to understand that your shoulders are built to wear this load, it will be easier for you to accept, even to the point where you may come to embrace it and, dare I say, enjoy it.

Should your shoulders grow weary, as they very well may at times, then you should know that the hands of your Heavenly Father have an insurmountable amount of strength. They are an everlasting resource to you if you'll reach out and grab them. Remember your strength comes from the creator of strength and since you are following in His footsteps, His resources are made readily available to you. But what's in this for you? If you learn to "take pride in your low position..." James 1:9 then your reward is great! There is, in fact, a payoff for your sacrifice. In verse 12 of that same chapter in James, he says:

> "Blessed is the one who perseveres under trial because having stood the test, that person will receive a crown of life..."

James is speaking in the spiritual sense but the same is true right here on Earth. Don't you think it is safe to say that if you can persevere through what may seem to be an inconvenience of your time on the weekend for the sake of investing in your family and therefore investing in yourself, that you will see a reward? The reward lies in your relationship with your wife that will be deepened and strengthened because of your commitment to investing time into it. The reward lies in the legacy of manly strength that you will leave in the hearts and minds of your boys, so much so that they will long to be like you or some version of you in order to lead their own homes one day. The reward lies in the hearts of your daughters. Because of your example they will filter out the seas of foolish men attempting to waste their time with lofty words. These men will not be given a chance because your daughters will have actually seen with their own eyes, and not only heard of the type of man they are looking for. Can you see it? Can you see your reward? Can you see your mother and or father so proud of their son that they are not even sure that they had anything to do with the way you turned out because they are so impressed? I can. That's the man I am trying to be. What about you? That's the man God is trying to make you into and, if all it takes is a little deliberate time and effort made towards the end goal of seeing your family "enriched", then it is so worth it! No sporting event, no amount of sleep, and definitely no amount of time with your homies is going to equal that kind of payoff. The funny thing is that, if you are deliberate about making time and not just "fitting in" your loved ones, then you'll probably have time for all those things as well.

You'll be surprised how much time there is in a day when you make it a point to plan the time you have. All of sudden you'll find all sorts of extra time to do extra stuff. My wife and I have been doing this for a while now and have found that it has significantly increased the time we have available to do the things we want and need to do in a crowded week, but, more importantly, it is helping us to create that enriched environment that we want for our kids and for each other. So go out and do the same thing. Creating time instead of just taking it when you can, pays exponentially.

CHAPTER ELEVEN
BE THE DAD YOU DIDN'T HAVE
DON,T BE THE VILLAIN.

All the great superheroes had absent parents in one way or another. Spider-Man's parents? Dead. Batman's parents? Dead. IronMan's parents? Dead. Are you noticing a pattern? Aside from the pattern of death, these characters all start from a place of despair because of no parental guidance. Now, whether your parents have physically passed or they were just emotionally dead to you while growing up, there is still hope for you. But let's just call a spade a spade and recognize that there are a lot of absent and horrible fathers out there in the world. I would probably say that there are more "bad" than "good" even. Thinking about this makes me want to hang my head in shame for my fellow gender mates. Somewhere along the lines of history we have lost our understanding of what true manhood is and what true fatherhood looks like. If we continue to do things the same way we will only perpetuate the cycle and leave future generations to suffer the repercussions of the decisions we make today. Just as Adam's decision not to rise up and be the man God created him to be affects us today, our decisions as men affect the future generations of men and women on this earth. So what do we do and where do we start?

IMAGINE A WORLD... (MOVIE GUY'S VOICE)

You start by imagining yourself to be that man you want to be. Be stronger than a locomotive; be faster than speeding bullets! I am verbally painting again but by now you should be able to get what I am saying. That imaginary man you see in your mind, that man of strength, honor, valor and wisdom, is the man you should strive for but you have to see him first before you can achieve being him. If you didn't have a picture of a father growing up it is time to let your imagination kick into overdrive. If you did have one then you have a head start. Many men have died in battle, and fought injustice in the name of being the men they imagined themselves to be so why should it be any different for you? It's not. Something worth having is always worth fighting for. Your fight may not be on a battlefield but will definitely be fought in your mind so be prepared to start there.

"...Write it down and make it plain..."

As the Bible says in Habakkuk 2:2, if God has given you a vision of biblical manhood then you should write it out. If He hasn't given it to you then I hope you are getting one from this read and you should still write it out. Give yourself a visual to strive for and put it somewhere you can see it on a regular basis. This is especially helpful if you are single but even more inspiring to your wife and kids if you have a family. Seeing Dad aspire to being a better and stronger man is almost better than actually being that superhero of a father. The visual, accompanied by action to support it, does great things in the eyes of children and wives. Not to mention the accountability that will come knowing that your wife and children are looking to you to see if you'll accomplish the goal you set before yourself.

Begin by writing out the qualities that would be evident in your most ideal vision of manhood. Pray over these things and pursue them recklessly. It will take time but it will be worth it. However, a word of caution. It's not enough to just pray or to just make an effort to become better. Too much prayer and not enough action will result in you being spiritually striking but physically lacking, which will, in turn, affect your spiritual life. Yet trying to pursue this without God being the center from which you draw strength is like trying put out a forest fire with only a water gun. It's only going to get you so far. Both are essential. In James 2:14-26, James outlines how important it is to combine your faith, we'll call it your vision for the type of man/father you want to be, with works, the actions that support your vision. James actually refers back to an older story of Abraham and says how, when Abraham used this formula, "it was accounted to him as righteousness," and that Abraham was called "the friend of God." Don't you want those two things to be said about you? I know I do.

You will notice I haven't said anything about actually succeeding in your vision. The effort made in preparation of a battle is more important than the battle itself because the result of the battle is a direct result of the preparation that has taken place. You can't get to your vision of that superhero if you don't do the things necessary to get you there.

A goal without a plan is just a wish. - Antoine de Saint-Exupery

I love the above quote because of the poignancy it offers. While "change" is good, it can be hard for us men to alter our own trajectories. Since men tend to think in compartments and be very good at task oriented direction, giving yourself a road map is not only a good idea, it's a great one. Simple bullet pointed directives allow us an achievable target by making the larger goals a bit more bite sized, while ambiguous goals set up us up for a fail because we lose interest and see them as too lofty or unobtainable.

So write out the man/father you want to be and place it somewhere you can see it daily. Somewhere you can pray over it, somewhere that allows you the ability to dream about it and even obsess over it a little before you step out into the world every day and then go get it! Pursue it with audacious tenacity, so much so that your efforts in it make you physically tired.

EXCUSES ARE NOT GETTING IT DONE

There are so many men out there in all cultures, in all societies making excuses as to the reason why they are not the men they should be. Things like they didn't have their own dad's example, they were raised by women, they came from a ghetto, they have the wrong skin color, they are the wrong race, they didn't have the money or perhaps having money was the issue. Maybe Mommy and Daddy had so much money that they loved the money more than they loved you. Who knows and, honestly, who cares? All excuses can be seen as valid to a degree, especially to the person giving them, and everyone has a reason why they can't do something, but it is the fathers and men who rise above the excuses and personal circumstances who achieve their goals and, in turn inspire, those around them especially their children. Find a way!

Excuses in the military get people killed and this is a war, gentlemen. Make no mistake about it, when you decide to be the man you didn't have in your life, you will face some battles. These battles will be external and internal. They will affect your mind, your body and soul. But giving way to the excuses of your past is like leaving the back door open to your mental fort. It gives a very real enemy access to your backside, which will impede any and all forward progress. If your vision is as big as the windshield of your car, you can't be stuck looking at the rear view mirror. You won't see where you are going, nor can you move forward. Kill all the excuses. Shut the back door and don't give the enemy a foothold to the battlefield of your mind! Forgive who you have to forgive. Cut all bad ties at the root and move forward. You have God given authority as a man. Use it! Don't deny it but operate in it. You don't have to be the biggest jock on the field to be strong. Strength is not measured in biceps, it's measured in precepts. It is measured in what we allow in and out of our minds, which, in turn, affects our lives. You can't change your past but you can change your future, so set your eyes on the horizon and plow ahead to the vision that God is giving you as a man and as a father.

JUST THE FACTS

If you didn't already know or understand how important it is that you get a vision for who you want to be as a dad, let me give you a few statistics to help. The following is a compiled list of stats found very easily on-line about the effect of fatherlessness in the home and how it directly affects children. However, because we are cutting out the excuses, I like to think of this list as a source of inspiration for why I need to have a vision for being a strong man and stronger father.

- 63% of youth suicides are from fatherless homes
  (US Dept. Of Health/Census)
  - 5 times the average.
- 90% of all homeless and runaway children are from fatherless homes
  - 32 times the average.
- 85% of all children who show behavior disorders come from fatherless homes
  - 20 times the average. (Center for Disease Control)
- 80% of rapists with anger problems come from fatherless homes
  - 14 times the average. (Justice & Behavior, Vol. 14, p. 403-26)
- 71% of all high school dropouts come from fatherless homes
  - 9 times the average. (National Principals Association Report)

Father Factor in Education - Fatherless children are twice as likely to drop out of school.

- Children with fathers who are involved are 40% less likely to repeat a grade in school.
- Children with fathers who are involved are 70% less likely to drop out of school.
- Children with fathers who are involved are more likely to get As in school.

- Children with fathers who are involved are more likely to enjoy school and engage in extracurricular activities.
- 75% of all adolescent patients in chemical abuse centers come from fatherless homes - 10 times the average.

Father Factor in Drug and Alcohol Abuse - Researchers at Columbia University found that children living in two-parent household with a poor relationship with their father are 68% more likely to smoke, drink, or use drugs compared to all teens in two-parent households. Teens in single mother households are at a 30% higher risk than those in two-parent households.

- 70% of youths in state-operated institutions come from fatherless homes
  - 9 times the average. (U.S. Dept. of Justice, Sept. 1988)
- 85% of all youths in prison come from fatherless homes
  - 20 times the average. (Fulton Co. Georgia, Texas Dept. of Correction)

Father Factor in Incarceration - Youths in father-absent households still had significantly higher odds of incarceration than those in mother-father families. Youths who never had a father in the household experienced the highest odds. A 2002 Department of Justice survey of 7,000 inmates revealed that 39% of jail inmates lived in mother-only households. Approximately forty-six percent of jail inmates in 2002 had a previously incarcerated family member. One-fifth experienced a father in prison or jail.

Father Factor in Crime - A study of 109 juvenile offenders indicated that family structure significantly predicts delinquency. Adolescents, particularly boys, in single-parent families were at higher risk of status, property and person delinquencies. Moreover, students attending schools with a high proportion of children of single parents are also at risk. A study of 13,986 women in prison showed that more than half grew up without their father. Forty-two percent grew up in a single-mother household and sixteen percent lived with neither parent.

Father Factor in Child Abuse - Compared to living with both parents, living in a single parent home doubles the risk that a child will suffer physical, emotional, or educational neglect. The overall rate of child abuse and neglect in single-parent households is 27.3 children per 1,000, whereas the rate of overall maltreatment in two-parent households is 15.5 per 1,000.

Father Factor in raising girls - Daughters of single parents without a father involved are 53% more likely to marry as teenagers, 711% more likely to have children as teenagers, 164% more likely to have a premarital birth and 92% more likely to get divorced themselves. Adolescent girls raised in a two-parent home with involved fathers are significantly less likely to be sexually active than girls raised without involved fathers.

- 43% of US children live without their father. [US Department of Census]
  - 90% of homeless and runaway children are from fatherless homes. [US D.H.H.S., Bureau of the Census]
- 80% of rapists motivated with displaced anger come from fatherless homes. [Criminal Justice & Behavior, Vol. 14, pp. 403-26, 1978]
- 71% of pregnant teenagers lack a father. [U.S. Department of Health and Human Services press release, Friday, March 26, 1999]
- 63% of youth suicides are from fatherless homes. [US D.H.H.S., Bureau of the Census]
- 85% of children who exhibit behavioral disorders come from fatherless homes. [Center for Disease Control]
- 90% of adolescent repeat arsonists live with only their mother. [Wray Herbert, "Dousing the Kindlers," Psychology Today, January, 1985, p. 28]
- 71% of high school dropouts come from fatherless homes. [National Principals Association Report on the State of High Schools]
- 75% of adolescent patients in chemical abuse centers come from

fatherless homes. [Rainbows for all God's Children]
- 70% of juveniles in state operated institutions have no father. [US Department of Justice, Special Report, Sept. 1988]
- 85% of youths in prisons grew up in a fatherless home. [Fulton County Georgia jail populations, Texas Department of Corrections, 1992]
- Fatherless boys and girls are: twice as likely to drop out of high school; twice as likely to end up in jail; four times more likely to need help for emotional or behavioral problems. [US D.H.H.S. news release, March 26, 1999]

As you can see, this is affecting our legacy. Our children are the ones who are suffering the most and who are responsible the least. What it also does is arm the next generation with their own set of excuses as to why they can't live out their full potential. If the excuses don't get them then stats will. It is so easy to glance over this list and not give it its proper attention. After all, these issues aren't new. Society knows that fatherlessness is a problem and is not surprised that it results in this type of behavior. However, the reason these things don't change is because not enough men care about this and are doing something about it. But if a man can make a bad decision and be affected by it many years later then the opposite must be true. If there is one man who will change the atmosphere in his circle of influence, the lives that can be touched are exponential. This is the power and influence of manhood and the anointing of a father. The power that we have been given is great and if we choose to exercise it properly then the affect is that much greater.

I think of great men who stood up throughout the course of history and fought injustices and how as a result of what these men did, we are still talking about them today. Men like Abraham Lincoln. He believed that enslaving another human being for the color of their skin was against God's given rights as free men and if we were to be a great nation we couldn't start by not valuing each other over something that is so insignificant. This was a counter-cultural ideology in the day. Martin Luther King's dream put him at the center of the Civil Rights Movement as well as many death threats. However he empowered not only African-Americans but the world to see that we are better united than we are divided. But arguably the greatest example of revolution in schools of thought and ideology was Jesus. This man, who lived over 2000 years ago, in the time span of three years, set in motion political and religious controversy that is still debated over today. He turned religious orthodoxy upside down by claiming he was the messiah and then acting like it was true. Even if you don't believe the claims that Jesus made about his deity, you have to recognize that the timeless messages he taught in such a short period of time affect everything in our modern life from time and season to politics and holidays. Jesus was bold in the face of adversity and, as males seeking to be men, we should be bold as well, whether that adversity comes from within ourselves or from the outside world.

Each of these men lived out their calls in spite of great opposition. One main thing that these three men have in common is that they were all killed for the stance that they took. As I was saying earlier, you will face adversity as each of these men did. You can't look at their deaths as defeat though. If anything, it was evidence that their messages had struck a nerve in the heart of people and some of those people didn't want things to change. Likewise, with you, it will be no different. You will meet opposition to your stance in both the physical world and the spiritual world. The enemy of your soul as well as some friends may think your new path is crazy because it is changing your perspective, vision and goals for your life. I think James says it best in James 1:2-4 (MSG):

> *"Consider it a sheer gift, friends, when tests and challenges come at you from all sides. You know that under pressure, your faith-life is forced into the open and shows its true colors. So don't try to get out of anything prematurely. Let it do its work so you become mature and*

well-developed, not deficient in any way."

I love that he says, *"So you will become mature and well developed..."* Don't we all want that? To be regarded as whole and complete, not lacking anything, especially when it comes to the "manliness" category. We want our women to worship us and our children to adore us but we have to be willing to put in the work to get it. The good thing is that, since we are men, we have been created for work. Though you may not have had the example of a father you want, you can work yourself towards becoming this man and—who knows?—maybe even better. Don't be the villain. Nobody likes that guy. Be the hero. Everyone loves him but more importantly, everybody needs him.

CHAPTER TWELVE
BE A GENTLENESS GIANT
LESS IS TRULY MORE.

In what is probably the most famous series of teachings that is recorded in the Bible, Jesus calls out the gentle and says that the whole earth belongs to them. The series, called "the beatitudes", gives us a straight-up list of doctrines to live by but I just want to look at one of them—the one that focuses on being gentle.

> *"God blesses those who are gentle. The whole earth will belong to them!"*
> *Mathew 5:5*

I think when you hear the word "gentle", it's probably that last thing you might associate with being masculine, manly or a hero. But don't we want that kind of blessing for our families? The kind of blessing that opens every door of opportunity and favor? Of course we do, so what does it actually mean to be gentle? Does being gentle mean to be weak? On the contrary, the truest strength is found in those who exhibit gentleness. Let me explain.

Gentleness is strength under control. A gentle person does not overreact, nor is he driven by his emotions. A gentle person is not someone who allows circumstances to dictate his behavior. The original word in the

Bible is actually is a Greek word. It's the word "Prautes" (prah-oo-tace), which literally means: a tamed wild stallion. And for this application the definition is dead-on. The image of a stallion is the epitome of unbridled strength and vigor. An untamed stallion in the wild contains tremendous strength; but strength that is uncontrolled is dangerous. Just like a wild stallion, without being taught to contain your strength, you can be dangerous too. As I have mentioned before, a fire in the fireplace can supply light and warmth, but a fire in the house can destroy everything that is precious to you. You can be a dangerous force to your loved ones and you can even be a danger to yourself. The difference in strength between the stallion in the wild and a stallion that has been tamed is nothing. They are both equally physically strong however, the horse that has been tamed has learned to control its strength for the master's use. This is strength under control. This is what it means to be gentle.

But how do we become gentle? How do we learn "strength under control"? Not in a sissy sort of way but in the way that demonstrates our God-given greatness. Let's take a look at a few practical ways we can get our strength under control or how being gentle can give us an advantage so that we, too, can be giants of gentleness.

USE GENTLENESS TO DIFFUSE CONFLICT

It so easy to react to a situation that seems to be out of control. It's even easier to mirror conflict when it approaches in order to establish dominance in a situation. But if we want to learn how to control our strength we have to learn to control our environment or, at the very least, control ourselves in that environment even when the environment seems uncontrollable. Gentleness is an antidote to anger. The Bible says it like this:

> *"A gentle answer turns away wrath, but a harsh word stirs up anger."*
> Proverbs 15:1 (NIV)

Did you know that you have a bio-mechanism built in the design of your brain that causes you to mimic the emotions of people across from you? They are called "mirror neurons". These cells give us the ability to empathize with others in our environment and allow us to feel and even reflect what they may be feeling or how they may be behaving. So, for instance, when you and your wife or girlfriend get into an argument where she may begin to raise her voice, your natural response is to raise yours higher. Then her response is to raise hers even higher. Then the cycle repeats because, in both of your minds, these neurons are firing. Can you see how this can be a dead-end cycle? How about if someone approaches you in a threatening manner? If the "fight" part of your fight or flight response kicks in, the same cycle may play out in a physical display of strength in efforts to, once again, establish dominance, but perhaps this time in the spirit of your own self-preservation. Either way, with the exception of a few cases, we cannot afford to lose our cool, even when the world around us is. Strength under control says that when emotions are high, you stay in control. When voices get high, you keep yours low.

> *"If your boss is angry with you, don't quit! A quiet, gentle spirit can overcome even great mistakes."*
> Ecclesiastes 10:4 (NLT)

Another reason why this is a good practice is because most people are not seeking to be out of control but as a result of the predicaments in their environment, they may be lashing out at you. They might be feeling pressure somewhere else in their life and you just so happen to be the one whom it is being taken out on. I didn't say it was fair, but if you respond with consistent gentleness while they are lashing out, how long do you think that argument will last? A fire does not grow when it is not fed and, in the same way, arguments calm down when someone takes control and does not allow them to grow by not feeding into them. A one-sided argument is just one person making a fool of themselves. Practice this type of control. When another person raises their voice, lower yours.

USE GENTLENESS TO DISARM CRITICS

The more successful you are in life, the more critics you will have. If you don't want any critics then don't do anything of any worth. In this day and age of social media, it is easy to get caught up in what the crowds think or what they say. Some of these folks are so dedicated to hating on others that they make a living at it. In some cases these people are even addicted to stirring up or being angry and, again, that has nothing to do with you or how you are living your life. So do not engage. Do not fuel the flame. Stay in control and move on.

Have you even seen the pointless conversations on social media that become a barrage of longer and longer retorts, each one trying to sound more educated and more long-winded than the previous response, just to make that person's point stand taller? What you are seeing is the digital version of what we have already discussed before. You are watching a virtual display of mirror neurons battling it out. Again, do not engage. This may be especially hard when the comments are directed toward us but you'll preoccupy so much less of your life and time by choosing to move on. By showing the strength of control, you are actually winning the argument. Not that winning is the goal, however being in control is. This is true gentleness on display. We want to have tough skin but a gentle heart.

> "We respond gently when evil things are said about us."
> 1 Corinthians 4:13 (NLT)

> "Your conversation should be so sensible that anyone who wants to argue will be ashamed because there won't be anything to criticize in anything you say!"
> Titus 2:8 (LB)

BE GENTLY PERSUASIVE

If you are a salesmen who has been in sales for some time, you'll know that the hard sell used to work. Whoever was the loudest, fastest, and most persistent would get the sale. However, in a day and age where the consumer is at the center of an á la carte smörgåsbord of options, the hard sell no longer works. If anything, when we feel someone is coming on too strong, we immediately push away. We think, This person has an ulterior motive and is trying to separate me from my money. I'm going to pass. Not 'cause I am not interested but because the pressure makes me second guess my purchase. The days of a hard sell are gone. But you know what does work? Gentleness. Consumers haven't gone away. We still buy stuff; we just do it on our own terms now. People buy now not because of hard pressing sales tactics but because of recommendations. Reviews and recommendations are now a part of every business's public relations/marketing team's concerns because it can literally make or break a brand. The brands, who have established transparency and make efforts to right the wrongs they commit against their customers, do their best in this digitally connected world because if they don't, the word gets out fast.

But is this new? Not really. The approach has just changed from hard to soft; from aggressive to gentle. People are still buying. They are just doing it on what they feel are their terms and, as consumers, we are more apt to buy something or from someone who isn't forcing themselves on us. Likewise, our approach to those around us must be the same. We cannot force our system of philosophy, way of doing things, or point of view for the sake of establishing dominance. We are more likely to push people away, but if we can learn to be gentle, people, especially our families, will be naturally attracted to us. People don't care how much you know until they know how much you care.

> *"Patience and gentle talk can convince a ruler and overcome any problem."*
> Proverbs 25:15b (CEV)

> *"A gentle word can get through to the hard-headed."*
> Proverbs 25:15b (NCV)

> *"A wise, mature person is known for understanding.*
> *The more pleasant his words, the more persuasive he is."*
> Proverbs 16:21 (TEV)

GENTLENESS MAKES US ATTRACTIVE

Did you know you attract what you are? If you are careless then you will attract careless people in your life. If you want your wife or girlfriend to be Godly then you must exhibit this behavior in your own life as well. We live in a generation of twisted and unparalleled expectations. We want our women to be fit supermodels, but we don't want to have to go work out ourselves. We want our children to display obedience but we haven't figured out how to be obedient to our bosses, much less our Heavenly Father. We want six figure salaries but not for the work we do. We want it to be for when we take breaks and vacations! We are backwards and in God's order it doesn't work. In the book of Timothy, Paul says this:

> *"As a man of God...pursue what God approves of:*
> *Godliness, Faith, Love, Endurance, and Gentleness."*
> 1 Timothy 6:11

In this letter to Timothy, Paul is encouraging a young man to be a great leader. The apostle Paul, at this point in his ministry, has seen firsthand what it takes to be successful in his calling as a leader and is now in a final farewell letter, passing on his legacy to the next generation. In the midst of his admonition, he throws in a curve. Alongside of all the other qualities that you might expect to be in the encouragement of a religious leader, he includes the pursuit of gentleness. It seems a bit odd because it doesn't have the God-like sound associated with it. It's not as religious sounding as other qualities like "Godliness", "Faith" or "Love". But there it is, right next to the big guns, hangin' tough. Paul equivocates the pursuit of gentleness right up there with Godliness. We should be quick to pay attention to this list if we want to be leaders in our homes and communities. These are the sorts of qualities that keep us attractive in the eyes of our wives, children and our followers.

GENTLENESS COMMUNICATES LOVE

If you want your wife and kids to be more responsive to you, speak to them gently, especially when it comes to speaking to your wife. In the book of Ruth, Ruth responds to Boaz's kindness by telling him how much she appreciated the way he spoke to her.

> *"...you have made me feel better because you have spoken gently with me..."*
> Ruth 2:13-14

As a result, the linage of King David is established through their relationship. This is the same linage that would lead to the birth of Christ. You can easily see how your gentleness could lead to greatness if you would only establish it in your home and in your demeanor with your wife. On the contrary, you never know what you could be missing out on by not speaking gently with her.

The sign of a great marriage is a union of two great forgivers. In order to forgive you have to come to terms with being great at being gentle. If it were only for the reason of needing forgiveness yourself, it would be enough, but if we want our loved ones to respond to us positively gentleness plays a key role here as well.

> *"Husbands, love your wives and be gentle with them."*
> Colossians 3:19 (NCV)

Gentleness extends to our children as well. We cannot set the bar so high in our expectations of them—though we may mean well—that our children are discouraged by them.

> *"Fathers, do not irritate and provoke your children to anger. Do not exasperate them to resentment, but rear*

> them tenderly in the training and discipline and counsel of the Lord."
> Ephesians 6:4 (Amp)

Gentlemen are gentle men. If we want to see a tangible effect of our gentleness, we need not look any further than our own homes. If you look around and don't see the home you want, remember all changes start with you and you can start by being gentle.

GENTLENESS EARNS RESPECT

Gentleness is a prerequisite of leadership. Every great leader understands the balance of authority and gentleness and how they play hand in hand. Dictators, however, rule by brute force and care not for tact or the well-being of those whom they hurt. This is not a superhero. This is a villain, a tyrant and no one wants to live under the rule of tyranny. They may obey you out of fear to your face but will hate and resent you behind your back. Leadership is already difficult enough. Do not make your job even harder by being a ruthless and careless leader.

BEING GENTLE IS A WITNESS TO UNBELIEVERS

Whether you realize it or not, nonbelievers are always watching you. If there is any doubt about this, check the comment sections of a controversial subject on any social media outlet. There you will find the open and often very vocal disagreements going on between Christians. You will also find one if not many comments of unbelievers mocking us as we disagree with each other publicly, saying things like, "This is why I am not a Christian," or "This is why I am no longer a Christian..." Our lack of unity in the public square speaks volumes about the ununited character of self-proclaimed Christians. It is not that we don't agree on certain subjects that is the problem, it's the lack of gentleness in how we speak to each other that communicates disrespect and a total lack of regard for the person on the other end of that comment thread. The arrogance is so pungent at times that I would almost have to agree with the critics of our faith while watching the verbal tennis matches that are going on. It's downright embarrassing and, from the outside looking in, not a motivator for our cause.

> "Believers should never speak evil of ANYONE, nor be quarrelsome. Instead they should be gentle and show courtesy to everyone."
> Titus 3:2 (GW)

> "Always be prepared to give an answer to everyone who asks you to give the reason for the hope that you have. But do this with gentleness and respect . . ."
> 1 Peter 3:15 (NIV)

We need to be the type of men who are pro-people. What I mean is this: There are many things out to divide us, and by "us" I mean humanity. Our religious world-view, our political world-view, our education, our race, our financial bracket, the type of work we do, etc.; these are all things people use to measure one another's worth. These are the gages people use to qualify each other and to see if the person on the other end is worth listening to. However, this is to our detriment. We cannot afford to add a lack of gentleness to a growing list of reasons why people will or will not listen to what we have to say. If we are to be examples to the world around us as representatives of Christ then at some point you are going to rub someone the wrong way. Some of those people just may be folks who say they believe the same thing you do. The key to maintaining our witness is in how we respond to their adversity. We have already gone over how to respond to opposition in point number one but in this case let me add this. Respecting all people no matter what world-view they hold is as much a part of being gentle as is not compromising on your own. You can quote scripture to a non-believer all day long, but if they don't see it in your life, what good is it? If anything, it stands to drive a wedge deeper between that person and Christ. The Bible says that YOU are the hands and feet of Christ. You are doing the work, but it is work that the unbeliever must see in your life if we ever want to reach them for the cause of Christ. Gentleness must be a visible part of your character because people are always watching and they are far more impressed with how you live than what you say.

GENTLENESS MAKES YOU LIKE JESUS

If you want to be like Christ in any way you have to learn the qualities that make up his character. Gentleness is one of them.

> *"Come to me, all you who are weary and burdened, and I will give you rest. Take my yoke upon you and learn from me, for I am gentle and humble in heart, and you will find rest for your souls."*
> Matthew 11:28-29 (NIV)

> *"The fruit of the Spirit is . . . gentleness!"*
> Galatians 5:22-23

Could it be that, if you are stressed out and tired all the time, you do not yet possess the gentleness that the Bible is talking about? The answer is yes. This is true because of a few reasons that we can see right there in the verse. The Bible's promise is an exchange of your man-made liabilities for God-made assets but it is contingent upon a few things so if you don't have the peace that the Bible is talking about, you know you are missing something.

You must first come to Christ. You must first submit your will to him to be like him. The first part of this verse says "Come to me..." If you are taking all your problems out on the world around you instead of taking them to the one who created the world, it will be easy to see how your influential reach might start to implode. But the good news is the second part of that first statement, "...all you who are weary and burdened..." Does that sound like you? Yes? Then you are in the right place. Secondly, the verse says this: "Take my yoke upon you and learn from me because I am gentle..." Jesus actually qualifies himself with the very thing we are in pursuit of with the statement "because I am gentle..." It is because Christ is gentle in his approach with us that he can, with authority, tell us that, if we trust and rely on his strength and not our own, we will get the peace we are seeking.

This is the type of strength that I want to exhibit in my life as a father. I know that so many times, I miss the mark on this one. I am grateful for the sensitivity of my wife, to gently set me back on course. Gentleness may not be something that is second nature to us men, but that is exactly why we need to learn how to establish it in our life. Men can be emotionally rough with each other and especially on themselves. However, when it comes to leading those who look to us for strength, being rough with them may not get us very far. Gentleness is more about finesse than it is strength. It is not about working harder with more fervor to show our prowess, it's about working smarter with more care to show our attention to detail. I don't know a woman or child alive who couldn't use a little more attention to detail when it comes from their dad. Being gentle doesn't make you small. It actually makes you a giant and in this case bigger is better.

CHAPTER THIRTEEN
WHAT *NOT* TO DO
KRYPTONITE ALERT

So far we have discussed several ways to improve your skills while attempting to be a hero in your house. Maybe you are not new to the parenting game. Maybe like Mr. Incredible you've been in the game for a long time and you just want to sharpen up your skills to remind yourself that you still got it. Either way, you are a student of this subject and sometimes when trying to understand a concept it is just as beneficial to look at the subject from alternate perspectives. This small list of things to do is by no means comprehensive, nor is this book meant to be. However, in an attempt to be as well rounded as I can in covering this broad topic, I want to also take a look at a few things that, as fathers, we should not do, in order to strengthen the things we should.

In Ephesians chapter 6, there is an outlined structure for the Christian family to follow. The whole book actually points to the distinction we are to have as believers from the rest of the world in various aspects of life. We are to live in light not darkness. We are to live in wisdom not foolishness. We are to walk in the Spirit not the flesh. We are to be sanctified or otherwise, separate or set apart from the way that the secular world views life and Ephesians chapter 6 explains how to do it. The chapter is deliberate in its direction and in raising children and running a home, there are no exceptions.

As previously mentioned in other chapters, the idea of receiving counsel from people whose basis of comparison is not biblically grounded offers a foundation of wisdom built on human fallibility. In other words, the methods of raising children offered by the world, while they may be well intended, are riddled with unforeseeable problems because they are limited in their human scope. They say, "Based on what we can see now, we think these antiquated methods do not work so let's try something else that is a little less offensive." Secular wisdom is not concerned with the future or eternity but Godly wisdom is. Secular wisdom is only concerned with the immediate. It says, "If it doesn't hurt anyone that I can see, if it doesn't offend anyone that I know of, if it is as neutral as possible, then it must be good and correct." However, history and stats say otherwise. There is much to learn from secularism. I am not discounting the wisdom of the world but what I am saying is that it is short sighted and incomplete in its analysis of how to live life.

In Leviticus chapter 18 God sets up a standard of behavior for the Israelites at the time. He says,

> *"You shall not do what is done in the land of Egypt where you lived, nor are you to do what is done in the land of Canaan where I am bringing you. You shall not walk in their statutes. You are to perform My judgments and keep My statutes and to live in accord with them."*

In other words, you're different. You are not to do things the way the world does. You are not to conduct your lives or your relationships the way the Egyptians do. Later in the same chapter, God says:

> *"Do not defile yourselves by any of these things, for by all these the nations which I am casting out before you have become defiled. Thus you are to keep My charge, or My command, that you do not practice any of the abominable customs which have been practiced before you so as not to defile yourself with them. I am the Lord your God."*

The truth of being separate and different in how we run our lives in the modern day isn't that much different. In verse 4, fathers are given a specific instruction,

> "And, fathers, do not provoke your children to anger but bring them up in the discipline and instruction of the Lord."

We need to come to terms with this in pursuing the "how" of being a good dad. What does it mean to "not provoke your children"? Though initially it may sound like a modern school of thought on raising children, it is not. We know that we are to be different from the world so our response to raising children is equally distinct.

First we must recognize where children come from and why they exist. The Bible says that children are given to us by God to be heritage and that they are a gift. I think this is evident by the fact that so many do not, or more specifically, *cannot* have children. They are given to us to be a symbol of praise and a sign of God's best directed towards our lives. If you do not have a relationship with Christ you may not be able to see this. If you have accepted Christ into your life but do not feel this way about children it is imperative that you learn about the parallels in your relationship with children and God's relationship with you. Though the Bible calls children a blessing and a heritage, how often are children seen only as a nuisance or a heartache, even by Christian people? The reason for this is that the parents are far too often not following the divine standard established by God in order that joy and blessings can be experienced; not only in the parents' lives but in the children's as well.

The instruction in verse 4 may sound like it is only directed at fathers but sometimes the word "fathers" is translated as "parents". This instruction cannot exclude the roles of mothers but is inclusive to both parents. Both parents, though unique in their individual roles, share responsibilities in the upbringing of children. You might say that the biblical standard of parenting is outdated. For example, when the apostle Paul is writing, he is writing these letters in the ancient Roman world dominated by the rule of fathers. In fact, there is a term they used to describe the established role that fathers had as dictators in their home. It was called "Patria Potestas", which means "Father's Power". This type of a fathering allowed the father to basically have ultimate control of his children's lives, even unto death if the father deemed necessary. He could rightfully and lawfully execute his own children if he felt it necessary to do so. As long as the father lived, there was no extent or limit to his control. Many children were disregarded at birth for being malformed or for simply being female. They would be thrown out onto the street to either die or be picked up as prostitutes or slaves.

Viewing this world, far removed by time, might make it easy to raise ourselves on a proverbial pedestal and believe that we have come far from this barbaric form of population control or male dominance, but it doesn't take much research to realize that we are no different from the ancient world of Rome that Paul is writing in. In our world today we don't wait till children are born to disregard them. We kill millions of them every year before they are even born and the ones who are allowed to be born are consequently beaten, burned and abused by their parents. About a million and half kids every year are removed from their families as a result this type of treatment and these are just the incidents that are being reported. Many children aren't fortunate enough to make it into "the system" because they are killed by their parents. They are drowned, thrown out of windows or off of bridges, stabbed to death, beaten with hammers or cut up with razor blades.

Our world today is in no way different from the ancient world. A recent survey in Time magazine reported that 70 percent of parents given the opportunity to be parents again would not have children because they are too much of a nuisance. It is no longer safe to be a child but maybe it never was. Somewhere around fifty-thousand children every year are used for child pornography, a third of all born children end up in foster homes, even more are left at home to be raised by televisions because mothers are out working to provide for families. Even President Obama recently signed into law a document that prevented the block of late term abortions. It is very safe to say that the modern world is against children just as much as the ancient world; and equally barbaric.

Paul's call to parents in the ancient world is the same and as relevant to modern day parents raising a child today. An old Harvard study by sociologists Sheldon and Eleanor Glueck identified four critical factors in preventing delinquency in children. First, a father's discipline must be fair, firm and consistent. Second, the mother's supervision over the home must allow her to know where the children are at all times and she must be available to her children. Third, the parents must show unending affection to each other and to the children frequently. Finally, the family must spend time together and show some sense of cohesiveness. Both parents have to be involved for this to be complete and it was found that when these elements come together there is a 90% success rate.

If you will notice, there is a both a negative and then a positive in the instruction Paul gives. Let's look at both. The negative says this: "Don't provoke your children to anger." The point of parenting your children is not to make them mad or angry. You don't want them to be hostile or bitter against you and all that is important to you. Do not do things that will irritate, frustrate or exasperate them; at least not for the sake of just doing these things. There are so many children in this day and age who are incredibly angry. I am not even talking about grown up children who have had a chance to process their childhood. I am speaking about very young children, as young as six and seven years old, being admitted to psychiatric wards because they have been contemplating and attempting suicide. A quarter of the admissions to the psychiatric units of children's hospitals are suicide related.

There was a recent report of a young child cutting his wrist. When questioned as to why he would do such a thing, he responded by saying:

> "I want to go to heaven, I can't stand these stomach aches and being unhappy. If only I could die, it's hard to live, living is horrible, I just want to die because nobody cares if I die so I just want to die."

Other children have been known to deliberately swallow poison or to run out into oncoming traffic. One young lady cut both of her legs with scissors, slashed her wrist, drugged her younger sister and overdosed on drugs. She was cited stating:

> "I would be better off dead, then no one will ever have to look at my ugly face again."

Another young boy tried to kill his dog, attempted to suffocate his baby brother with a pillow and jabbed pins and needles into his stomach. He said it was because *"Mother doesn't have any love in her for me."* The examples are numerous, everywhere and are easy to find.

Perhaps what you are doing as a parent may not be what's causing these types of problems. It might just be what you don't do for them that could lead to issues. How can you provoke your children to anger? How can you turn your child into a tragedy? Here are some things Pastor John MacArthur lists that you might be doing to provoke your children. You probably don't realize that you are doing these things and you probably don't want to do them either.

> -**Spoil him.** *Give him everything he wants, even more than you can afford, just charge it so you can get him off your back.*
>
> -*When he does wrong, nag him a little but* **don't spank him.**
>
> -**Foster his dependence on you.** *Don't teach him to be independently responsible.*

-*Maintain his dependence on you* so later on drugs and alcohol can replace you when he's older.

-*Protect him from all those mean teachers* who want to discipline him from time to time. And threaten to sue them if they don't let him alone.

-*Make all of his decisions for him* because he might make mistakes and learn from them if you don't.

-*Criticize the other parent*, so your son or daughter will lose respect for his parents.

-*Whenever he gets into trouble, bail him out.* Besides, if he faces any real consequence, it might hurt your reputation.

-*Never let him suffer the consequences of his behavior.* Always step in and solve his problems for him so he will depend on you and run to you when the going gets tough and never learn how to solve his problems.

-*If you want to turn your child into a delinquent,* **let him express himself anyway he feels like it.**

-*Don't run his life*, let him run yours.

-*Don't bother him with chores.* Do everything for him then he can be irresponsible all his life and blame others when things don't get done right.

-*And be sure to give in* when he throws a temper tantrum.

-*Believe his lies* because it's too much hassle to try to sort through to get the truth.

-*Criticize others openly* and routinely so that he will continue to realize that he is better than *everybody else.*

*-**Give him a big allowance** and don't make him do anything for it.*

*-**Praise him for his good looks**, never for character.*

If you want a child to fall into the category of tragedy just ignore him and watch him hurt himself to get your attention.

Let me also give you a list of things NOT to do in order to avoid provoking your children to anger.

OVERPROTECTION

If you never trust them or give them an opportunity to develop their own sense of independence it will instill a spirit of resentment. Kids gradually need room to express themselves, discover and venture out. Christians have a tendency to do this with the intention of protecting our children from the grasp of the enemy and the evil that awaits their entrance into the world. What we fail to realize is that evil was born in them and from the beginning that seed existed in their heart. You don't have to teach a child to misbehave. You have to teach them what is right but forcing it on them by not giving them a chance to experience anything else will suffocate and leave the child feeling frustrated.

FAVORITISM

Favoritism for one child over another is a quick way to discourage a child and to force him into doing something to get an equal amount of attention whether it be positive or not. Isaac favored Esau over Jacob; Rebekah favored Jacob over Esau. The results are well-known. You cannot compare children because, much like our thumb prints, they are all different. Love them the same with regard for each and without special regard for one over the an other. If a child feels that you love another sibling more than you love them you could find that child extremely frustrated in trying to get your attention and you may not know where it comes from.

UNREALISTIC GOALS

James Dobson has a teaching series called "Shaping the Will Without breaking the Spirit" and in regards to setting goals for your children, I believe he hit the nail on the head. Our goal as parents is to equip our kids with the best tools for the unique and individualized road ahead. That requires a lot of molding and shaping of an individual will. But it is important that our touch be light and lead by the natural inclinations of the child. Vicariously living out our own life's dreams through their lives could add a severe amount of unnecessary pressure in their hearts. It could potentially lead the child to be angry, distant and bitter towards you for making them pursue goals that were not their own.

GIVING THEM EVERYTHING

Though this one may be a bit more elusive, you could easily frustrate your child by giving in to their every whim. Every passing fad, sports team, hobby or clothing trend may be drawing your child's attention but just because they want it all doesn't mean you give it all to them. You might always be cleaning up after them or allowing them to pass responsibility off to others so that they don't have to own the repercussions of their actions. You might say you are doing this in the name of "helping them out" but help them out one too many times and you may find a child who is far more dependent that you want him to be. One day these kids will grow up and realize that the world is not going to own their responsibilities and by not setting them up for a healthy expectation of what responsibility looks like, you have crippled them. It could make them extremely angry and bitter.

DISCOURAGEMENT

Children are vacuums for approval. They thrive on it and need it constantly and sincerely. As parents we must be available to them with a listening ear and a gracious heart. They are going to make a ton of mistakes along the way but haven't we all, both in childhood and adulthood? I think it is important to remember that our relationship with our earthly children is a reflection of our relationship with our Heavenly Father. When I think about how God handles my discouragement I am quickly reminded of how He does not avoid chastising me but He is gentle in restoring me. I want to parent like that. I want make sure I have an understanding of each of my children's uniqueness and the uniqueness of their individual purposes in life. This can help me see circumstances that surround them and how to assess them a little more clearly and judiciously. I want to be firm and fair without defeating and discouraging.

MAKING THEM AN INCONVENIENCE

For some people, having children is an awaited moment that they were ready to embrace. Yet for others, it was a dreaded task that can only be endured. For both sets of folks, there are times when it's all you can do just to hold on and wait till the moment passes but it is those who make a life out of treating their children this way that are in danger of angry adult children. People who retain the mindset of their single-hood into parenthood have a tendency to do what they want to do and go where they want to go and most likely that is without the "distraction" of their kids. But thinking of your kids as a "distraction" will lead you to behave in a way that will alienate them and they will soon catch on. Leaving children in the care of others who do not care for them as a parent should or leaving them to fend for themselves on a regular basis could be building a foundation of resentment that will be directed towards you at a later date.

NOT LEAVING ROOM FOR MISTAKES

Ever notice how the face of a child lights up if you tell them you really need their help with something? It's like there is a sense of pride that they take in being needed for assistance. Perhaps they think to themselves, "Why would someone so big need the help of someone so small? It doesn't even matter. I can do it!" Maybe they don't, but whatever the case may be, that little seedling of a person is going to grow and their childhood is a chance for them to practice being an adult. They are being given an opportunity to spread their wings and see what they are good at and what they are not so good at so it might be clear to some parents that they are going to make mistakes. Yet for others, there might be a tendency to hold kids to such a high standard that it doesn't give them room to make mistakes. For a parent, giving your kids room to grow is extremely scary. After all, what if they like it and don't need us anymore? We may run the risk of them never coming back, right? Well, the reality is that they are never truly ours to begin with. They are gifts that we only have for a time. They are meant to leave. The time we have with them is short and, though there will be plenty of time for fun, there must also be an equal amount of time learning to be an adult. Isn't that what we are doing from the moment they are born anyways? Since the moment of conception we are quite literally training them to stand on their own and be their own person. If we are not careful we can easily stand in the way of that progress and think that we are doing them a service when, in reality, we are just provoking their anger against us. We should expect progress not perfection. They should be able to fail, especially if necessary, and not fear that your approval will be affected by their failure.

NEGLECT

Oftentimes, when we think of neglected children, it may be easy to think of the things that are more obvious in terms of neglect. For example it's easy to look at a child and see the visual signs that would categorize them as physically neglected, malnourished or abused. What is not so easily visible is if a child has been emotionally neglected, especially in the area of consistent loving discipline. When these types of neglect manifest themselves, the repercussions can be just as devastating to look at. Consistent discipline sets a standard of expectation that children are inherently looking for. This type of discipline cannot be administered without a proper balance of love and relationship with the child, lest you be looked at as a stranger. The discipline of a father who has invested time in a child, who loves, cares and shows physically that he loves and cares, is a discipline that is highly regarded by a child even if in the moment it may not seem so.

ABUSIVE WORDS

Many people do not believe in physically spanking children but what could be far more damaging are the sharp words of sarcasm, anger and ridicule that a parent may opt for when looking to dole out some kind of punishment instead of spanking children. It's easy to say things to our children that we would never say to anyone else because there is no apparent repercussion. However, there are grave repercussions if we do not learn to control what comes out of our mouths.

PHYSICAL ABUSE

Lastly, children can easily end up angry as the result of physical abuse. Parents who are over-zealously punishing a child are usually angry themselves. This type of punishment is coming from a parent who feels as though they have been inconvenienced or irritated and not that the child needs correction for his own good. Dealing out a punishment in this mind state, as a parent, is a horrible idea that can further drive the child into rebellion rather than submission. In fact, the idea of discipline should probably not be looked at as trying to get a child to "submit" as opposed to having a child "in training" who sometimes may need some redirecting.

There you go. Ten things not to do unless you want to deliberately provoke your child to anger and weaken your superhero powers in your home. Instead of doing these things, the negative part of the verse, focus on the positive part of the verse. "...bring them up in the discipline and instruction of the Lord." The implication here is that they need you to do this. YOU "bring them up". The instruction is a call to action for both parents. Children cannot do it alone. They need you. Proverbs 29:15 says,

"A child left to himself brings his mother shame."

As I said earlier, it is not what we do as much as what we don't do that can drive a child to anger. So, while adding all of the skills mentioned in this book to your super-dad regimen, make sure you are dropping this list of behaviors from your parental practice. Heroes cannot afford to only be great at all the easy stuff. The hard stuff is actually where the true tests of heroism lies.

THE FINAL CHAPTER
A LEAGUE OF EXTRAORDINARY GENTLEMEN SURRENDER IT ALL AT THE CROSS.

> *"A journey of a thousand miles begins with a single step"* - Chinese philosopher Laozi

I am not sure where you are on this journey or how it is you came about my scribblings on how to be a better dad, but I do know that, however it was, it was not by chance. There is a greater purpose that we are all serving and being a hero in your home is a significant piece of this purpose. A father I respect sat me down one day and said to me:

"Rick, you have two callings in this life. One is a low calling and the other is a high calling. It is up to you to find your low calling, or what you choose to do on Earth with your time that has earthly or temporal value. However, at the same time you should also be fulfilling your high calling or the calling that comes from God. These are the tasks that have eternal value."

May I present to you, gentlemen, that being a father is a bit of both. You may feel that you stumbled upon fatherhood or that you were not ready to be a dad. You may feel that you are just fumbling your way through it and that sometimes you have to just close your eyes and hold your breath until the moment is over. You may feel that the low and earthly calling of being a father is not as significant in the grand scheme of eternal life or that what God has planned for you to do will affect people's destinies. However, believing these things would mean buying into a huge set of lies. Your low, or earthly, calling is one of great significance that has ripple effects that are far beyond what the eyes can see in the minute amount of time that we are given on this planet. This is why it is also a high calling or a heavenly calling. The role of leadership and fatherhood are mandates given to you and they were set in motion from the day of your own conception. You did not choose it but it was gifted to you. It was not given as a result of your own merit or sense of self-worth but a free gift for you to steward over and guard carefully. So how will you use it? Will you squander it and allow the weeds of life to choke any or all potential you have to leave a strong legacy with your children and your children's children? Or will you assert yourself in a capacity that says you are giving your best efforts to making your impact great?

You are not a dad just because you have, or are planning to have, children. You consciously own that title by doing the things that allow you to claim it. There are plenty of men who are clearly opting out both physically and mentally. You did not have to read this book either, but assuming you did read it, or some portion of it, I think it would be safe to say that you are searching for tools to be the best dad you can be. You are searching for a deeper sense of what exactly your calling is or how to navigate it successfully and that is a sign of great strength. That is a sign of being an epic father and a hero in the home.

In every young boy there is a seed of greatness and a seed of disgrace. Whichever seed is watered, nurtured and cultivated more throughout the course of his life will be the one to sprout into fruition in his adult years. I am not sure what has been cultivated in your life. Only you can truly tell that story. However, wherever you find yourself, I want you to know that finding out where you need to go comes in the form of surrendering it all at the feet of a man named Jesus. He is the most controversial figure of all time and remains to be a subject of great study and debate. His life was brief but the life he led and the teachings that surround him are of infinite worth in many areas but especially in being a great dad. The time tested principles outlined in his story, along with the great truths found only in the Bible, are the keys to understanding who we are to be as men. They should be pursued feverishly and without relent. We should learn to feast at the table of knowledge that knowing Christ and understanding the Bible can provide. It is a long and deep journey, one that is treacherous most of the way but also one that is richly rewarding.

Not having it all figured out is OK if you do have this one thing understood—the answers to life's toughest questions lie in the Creator of all things. I have many times in the course of my life fallen victim to the traps that my mind has set, things like managing life and figuring out how to be the man I am supposed to be in my own strength. Being in the middle of all of that can be a daunting task. Many men have literally not made it through alive and after having lived it for only a short while, I can easily see why. There are traps all around us, gentlemen, and unfortunately many of our fellow soldiers are being picked off. Many of them are falling victim to their own free will. It is a shame and a disgrace to the gender.

In a time long since gone, old men used to be honored and revered for carrying the prestigious title of "father". Now, men are shunned and disregarded for that very same title but not without cause. Years of neglecting the responsibilities that come with the label of "father" have reproduced generations of young boys and girls who have not only perpetuated the cycle of neglect, but have also lost the vision for what true manhood looks like. Still, every day is a chance to stop the continuation of this cycle in the lives of your children. But you must embrace those chances by realizing that we can't do it without God's help and then taking action.

Trying to figure out the "how" in all of this can leave a man in a maddening state. Every man wants to be great at anything he puts his hands to. I have never met a man who wanted to deliberately be bad at anything he did. But somewhere along the way if a man is beaten down enough, he will believe he cannot be amazing because, apparently, he doesn't know how to be great. I have had many of my fathering questions answered by surrendering them at the foot of the cross of Jesus Christ. If you are not familiar with what this great man has done for each of us to have access to these answers, please get a Bible, in a translation that makes it easy for you to understand, and read the following verses: Romans 3:10-12, and 23, 6:23, 5:8, 10:9-10, and 13. And for every question that has not been answered as a result of the previously mentioned verses, choose to lay down a spiritual brick of faith. It is a brick that says, "Just because I don't know the answers right now, does not mean that the answers do not exist." It also says, "Because of the sacrifice that was made on a Roman cross two thousand years ago, I can trust today that my entire life and all the decisions therein are in good hands even unto death." These types of mental and spiritual bricks have served to build up a wall of faith not only for my life but for the lives of men who, just like me, are trying to figure it all out. This wall creates a divide in my mind. It separates the world of unanswered questions relating to the "How I should be a great dad" and the "Who is making me a great dad". The "How" is not as important as the "Who". The "Who" is the Father of all Fathers. The Alpha and Omega, the beginning and the end. It all starts and ends with Him. He is the God who possesses the answers we are seeking.

I am grateful for the journey He has given me even if I have been bruised and broken along the way. It is only when I truly lay my life in the Creator's hands that the questions of life and how to be a great dad do not seem so overwhelming because I know that He is in control and working for my good. When I allow total surrender of my will, my mind and my confusion to the God who has all the answers, only then am I given a clear vision of how to be the man I am trying to be. Only then does He make my crooked paths straight and restore the years that the locusts have eaten away from my life. And for you it will be the same. When you give over your heart and will, when you give Jesus Christ an all-access pass to your vulnerabilities then He will give you a clear line of sight on how to be a hero in your home.

> *What's a father?*
> *He's strength and security, laughter and fun,*
> *A prince to his daughter, a pal to his son.*
> *A great story-teller and mender of toys,*
> *Who's seldom dismayed by his family's noise.*
> *He's an everyday Santa who brings home surprises,*
> *The man to consult when a problem, arises.*
> *As eager a worker as ever there'll be*
> *Who wants all the best for his whole family.*
> *He's a loving instructor who struggles to teach*
> *His child to achieve all the goals one could reach.*
> *And he knows in his heart that it's worth all the bother*
> *When he hears his child say, "That man? That's MY father!"*
>   *-author unknown.*

Ricardo Navarro is a Christian author who seeks to motivate and inspire a generation with thought-provoking and creative commentary that challenges people to not only love God with their heart, soul and strength but to love Him fully and completely with their minds. Rick is gratefully married to Diona Navarro and has been for 6 years. They have 3 children; Peighton (10), Greyson (3) and Jace (2). The Navarro family lives in Southern California.

Ricardo can be reached by email at thecrazychristianblog@gmail.com.

Printed in Great Britain
by Amazon